Penguin Masterstudies
Joint Advisory Editors:
Stephen Coote and Bryan Loughrey

The Poetry of
William Wordsworth

Alan Gardiner

Penguin Books

Penguin Books Ltd, Harmondsworth, Middlesex, England
Viking Penguin Inc., 40 West 23rd Street, New York, New York 10010, U.S.A.
Penguin Books Australia Ltd, Ringwood, Victoria, Australia
Penguin Books Canada Limited, 2801 John Street, Markham, Ontario, Canada L3R 1B4
Penguin Books (N.Z.) Ltd, 182–190 Wairau Road, Auckland 10, New Zealand

First published 1987

Made and printed in Great Britain by
Richard Clay Ltd, Bungay, Suffolk
Typeset in 9/11 pt Monophoto Times

Contents

Note to the Reader

Unless otherwise stated, all quotations are from *William Wordsworth: The Poems* (Volumes 1 and 2), edited by John O. Hayden (Penguin, 1977). The chapter on 'The Prelude' is based upon the 1805 text, edited by Ernest de Selincourt and Stephen Gill (Oxford University Press, 1970). Line numbers have been given when quoting from lengthy poems but have usually been considered unnecessary for quotations from shorter works.

1. The Poet and His Age

The attempt to date and define the so-called Romantic movement in English poetry is a notoriously difficult exercise. At one time it was considered convenient to regard the publication of Wordsworth and Coleridge's *Lyrical Ballads* in 1798 as the starting-point of English Romanticism, with the death of Byron in 1824 marking its end. However, much of the finest work of William Blake (who is always regarded as one of the movement's most important figures) pre-dates 1798 by several years, and some of the characteristics most commonly associated with Romantic verse – the intense feeling for nature and the interest in older forms of literature, for example – are found in still earlier poets. Moreover, verse similar in attitude, subject-matter and style to that of the leading Romantic poets continued to be written after 1824. We ought therefore to recognize the dangers involved in identifying Romanticism too closely with a specific period in literary history. There remains, however, the further problem of determining exactly what we mean by Romanticism. The reference in the opening sentence to the Romantic 'movement' might be taken to imply the existence of a collection of writers united by agreed ideas and objectives. In fact the poets of the late eighteenth and early nineteenth centuries differ greatly (often very greatly) in their beliefs and intentions and were certainly not conscious of themselves as members of a recognizable literary group. They became known as Romantics retrospectively – in the 1860s – and it is only in the twentieth century that 'Romanticism' has come into use as a term for a particular set of opinions on thought, emotion and art.

These necessary qualifications should not however prevent us recognizing that the closing decades of the eighteenth century and the first thirty or forty years of the nineteenth are marked, in continental Europe as well as in Britain, by a major shift in literary theory and practice. The poets of the period do tend to have certain attitudes in common, though these attitudes are invariably present in some poets rather than in all, and where they are present vary considerably in degree. This chapter will seek to outline some of these attitudes, concentrating upon those which enhance our understanding of Wordsworth's poetry in particular. It will also give a brief account of Wordsworth's life, focusing again on those biographical details which shed some light on the poems. Our knowledge of an author's personal history should not so prejudice our response to his work that our understanding of it is distorted rather than enriched, but a certain amount of biographical information is of particular use to the reader of a poet such as Wordsworth, whose work draws so much upon his own life – upon the experiences of his childhood, the growth of his imagination, his changing political opinions and his complex relationship with the natural world.

The period in which Wordsworth and his fellow Romantic poets wrote was one of political and economic upheaval. Politically, it was a time of revolutions in America and France; in Britain revolution was averted but the demand for constitutional change eventually resulted in the Reform Act of 1832. Economically, however, Britain led the world in another kind of revolution: the Industrial Revolution, which was at its height during the age of Romanticism. Society became increasingly reliant upon mass production, and there was a shift of population towards the factories of the North and the Midlands. In the countryside, an agricultural revolution was also taking place. Under the old open-field system of farming landholders cultivated strips of arable land and had access to large areas of common land for pasture. During the eighteenth and early nineteenth centuries land became consolidated into private enclosed farms. Enclosure transformed the rural environment; meadows, woodlands and wastes disappeared, and were replaced by a new pattern of fences, hedges and walls. Whereas before a high proportion of the population of a village shared in the ownership of the land, the enclosed farm was the property of a large landowner, and cultivation was carried out by the landless labourer working for a wage. There was thus a steady erosion of the small, independent landholder. Dorothy Wordsworth records in her Journal a conversation on this topic with a Lake District neighbour in 1800:

John Fisher overtook me on the other side of Rydale. He talked much about the alteration in the times, and observed that in a short time there would be only two ranks of people, the very rich and the very poor, for those who have small estates says he are forced to sell, and all the land goes into one hand.

The old society, based upon small, close-knit communities, was threatened by industrial and agricultural developments alike. Wordsworth expressed his concern in 1817: 'the principal ties which kept the different classes of society in a vital and harmonious dependence upon each other have, within these thirty years, either been greatly impaired or wholly dissolved'.

This background of massive social and economic change helps to explain the Romantic enthusiasm for nature. The countryside was valued because it was seen as superior to the grim environment of the growing industrial towns. There was a particular admiration for those parts of nature that had not been shaped and ordered by human intervention; mountains are a recurring symbol of beauty and mystery in Romantic verse. Another aspect of the reaction against industrialism was a nostalgia for simple rural society, for an environment in which people lived and worked in harmony with nature. There was a new interest in the attitudes and experiences of ordinary country people, because their way of life had not been corrupted by the artificialities of city life. In the Preface to *Lyrical Ballads* Wordsworth explains that he chose to write about 'low and rustic life' because 'in that situation the essential passions of the heart find a better soil in which they can attain their maturity'. In 'Michael' he pays tribute to the small landholders whose livelihood was threatened by the new economic developments. A letter to Charles James Fox explains his intentions:

I have attempted to draw a picture of the domestic affections as I know they exist amongst a class of men who are now almost confined to the North of England. They are small independent proprietors of land, here called statesmen, men of respectable education who daily labour on their own little properties. The domestic affections will always be strong amongst men who live in a country not crowded with population, if these men are placed above poverty. But if they are proprietors of small estates, which have descended to them from their ancestors, the power which these affections will acquire amongst such men is inconceivable by those who have only had an opportunity of observing hired labourers, farmers, and the manufacturing poor. . . . This class of men is rapidly disappearing.

The regard for unspoilt, natural man led to a new interest in the insights of childhood, an interest that is most evident in the poetry of Wordsworth and Blake. Because their perception of the world had not been distorted by the conventions of adult society, children in a sense knew more than adults; in Wordsworth's Immortality Ode the child is addressed as 'Thou best Philosopher' and 'Mighty Prophet'. In 'The Prelude' Wordsworth recreates the central experiences of his earliest years and emphasizes the importance of adults retaining contact with their childhood self.

'The Prelude' is also the supreme example in Romantic poetry of the celebration of the individual consciousness (at one time it was to have been entitled 'A Poem on the Growth of an Individual Mind'). The Romantics' belief in the importance of personal experience can be seen as another reaction against the movement towards a mass society. In the

Preface to *Lyrical Ballads* Wordsworth observed that one consequence of urban civilization was the suffocation of the individual intellect:

A multitude of causes, unknown to former times, are now acting with a combined force to blunt the discriminating powers of the mind, and, unfitting it for all voluntary exertion, to reduce it to a state of almost savage torpor. The most effective of these causes are the great national events which are almost daily taking place, and the increasing accumulation of men in cities, when the uniformity of their occupations produces a craving for extraordinary incident, which the rapid communication of intelligence barely gratifies.

The new preoccupation with exploring individual experience is evident not only in the verse of the period but also in prose works such as De Quincey's *Confessions of an English Opium Eater* and Coleridge's *Biographia Literaria.* When the subject is not the writer himself it is often a character outside organized society; the solitary is a figure found again and again in Wordsworth's poetry – the leech-gatherer in 'Resolution and Independence', the Wanderer in 'The Excursion', the discharged soldier in 'The Prelude', the Old Cumberland Beggar.

Another manifestation of the Romantics' willingness to investigate forms of experience that the poets of the eighteenth century had largely neglected was their emphasis on the importance of the emotional life. The Augustans had favoured reasoned control of the emotions, but this attitude was firmly rejected by Blake:

Men are admitted into Heaven not because they have curbed and govern'd their Passions or have No Passions, but because they have Cultivated their Understandings. The Treasures of Heaven are not Negations of Passion, but Realities of Intellect, from which all the Passions Emanate Uncurbed in their Eternal Glory.

Wordsworth said the poet was an individual 'with more lively sensibility, more enthusiasm and tenderness ... than are supposed to be common among mankind' and declared that 'all good poetry is the spontaneous overflow of powerful feelings'. However, Wordsworth qualified the latter statement by asserting that poetry of value could be produced only by a poet 'who being possessed of more than usual organic sensibility had also thought long and deeply'. Although intensity of feeling is a characteristic of much of Wordsworth's best poetry he did not believe in the undisciplined expression of emotion. Rather, he maintained that poetry 'takes its origin from emotion recollected in tranquillity'. In the course of this recollection the poet's original experiences are meditated upon and subjected to a disciplined process of evaluation and selection.

Wordsworth believed that another essential attribute of the poet was imaginative power. Like other Romantic writers, he considered imagination the greatest of our faculties. While the neo-classical critics of the eighteenth century accepted that the imagination was capable of recalling images from the past and of forming new images by combining separate sense-impressions, the Romantics ascribed to it a much greater creative power. According to Romantic theory, the imagination interacts with the external world and in so doing transfigures it, so that the mind is (in Wordsworth's words) 'creator and receiver both'. The imagination enables us to 'see into the life of things' and to perceive invisible realities. In 'The Prelude' Wordsworth recalls the first intimations of this 'plastic power':

> *An auxiliar light*
> *Came from my mind on which the setting sun*
> *Bestow'd new splendor, the melodious birds,*
> *The gentle breezes, fountains that ran on,*
> *Murmuring so sweetly in themselves, obey'd*
> *A like dominion; and the midnight storm*
> *Grew darker in the presence of my eye.*

> Book II, ll. 387–93

The experiences of childhood were a recurrent source of inspiration for the adult poet. He had been born (on 7 April 1770) at Cockermouth in Cumberland, the second child in a family of four boys and a girl. His father, John Wordsworth, was an attorney employed by Sir James Lowther, later Earl of Lonsdale. Nature was an influence from his earliest years. The garden of the Wordsworth house ran down to the River Derwent:

> *That one, the fairest of all Rivers, lov'd*
> *To blend his murmurs with my Nurse's song,*
> *And from his alder shades and rocky falls,*
> *And from his fords and shadows, sent a voice*
> *That flow'd along my dreams.*

> 'The Prelude', Book I, ll. 272–6

When his mother died in 1778 he was sent to the grammar school at Hawkshead. He spent his free time exploring the Lake District countryside: ice-skating on the lake of Esthwaite, climbing the hills in search of birds' nests, fishing, rowing and horse-riding. These episodes are vividly recreated in Books I and II of 'The Prelude'. The boy enjoyed an intimate communion with the secret life of nature, but comprehension of the meaning and significance of his early experiences came only with adult reflection and meditation. As a child his mind 'Work'd with a dim and undetermin'd sense/ Of unknown modes of being', he listened to the wind's 'strange utterance' and scenes entered 'unawares into his mind'. During this period he was 'Foster'd alike by beauty and by fear'. Sometimes nature would fill him with awe and terror, as when he stole a boat and through an optical illusion had the impression that a huge mountain was pursuing him. At other times, 'from excess/ Of happiness, my blood appear'd to flow/ With its own pleasure, and I breath'd with joy'. But whether it induced fright or elation, the boy's environment was steadily shaping his consciousness, instilling both a respect for nature's separate life and a sense of the profound connections between humanity and the external world.

Wordsworth's father died in 1783, and along with his brothers and sister he came under the guardianship of their father's brother Richard and their mother's uncle Christopher Crackanthorp. His guardians hoped that he would eventually take up a career in the Church and in 1787 he was sent up to St John's College, Cambridge. In 'The Prelude' Wordsworth recollects that at Cambridge he had the dispiriting feeling that 'I was not for that hour,/ Nor for that place.' He had little enthusiasm for his academic course and graduated with a pass degree in 1791. But while he may have neglected parts of the prescribed course of study it is clear that during his student years he read avidly and benefited from what was in effect an intensive programme of self-education, one that far exceeded the scope of his university syllabus. His sister Dorothy observed that 'He reads Italian, Spanish, French, Greek, Latin and English, but never opens a mathematical book.' He was acquiring an intellectual vigour to complement the emotional sensitivity his earlier years had encouraged.

Moreover, he was now making a serious effort to write poetry. He had already written (probably in the spring and summer of 1787) 'The Vale of Esthwaite', much of which is conventional eighteenth-century landscape verse. In places, however, it anticipates the later poetry's interest in nature's capacity to exercise, through the workings of memory, an enduring influence:

> *No spot but claims the tender tear*
> *By joy or grief to memory dear.*

In his vacations from Cambridge he wrote his first poem of significance, 'An Evening Walk'. This was published in 1793 along with 'Descriptive Sketches', a poem inspired by visits to France and Switzerland in 1790 and 1791. 'An Evening Walk' describes a series of Lake District scenes.

It is typically eighteenth century in its form (heroic couplets) and its ornate diction. Wordsworth had not yet found his own distinctive voice, and the poem borrows heavily from such poets as Gray, Milton, Thomson and Pope. 'Descriptive Sketches' was similarly derivative. The conventional topographical verse of the eighteenth century, with its emphasis on pictorial description, was an inappropriate medium for a poet whose finest work would concern itself not with the objective representation of natural scenes but with the exploration of humanity's complex and varying response to its surroundings. A revealing note on a description of an Alpine sunset in 'Descriptive Sketches' indicates where his true interest in nature lay:

I had once given to these sketches the title of Picturesque; but the Alps are insulted in applying to them that term. Whoever, in attempting to describe their sublime features, should confine himself to the cold rules of painting would give his reader but a very imperfect idea of those emotions which they have the irresistible power of communicating to the most impassive imaginations . . . that controuling influence, which distinguishes the Alps from all other scenery, is derived from images which disdain the pencil.

When Wordsworth made his first visit to France in 1790 the spectacular scenery of the Alps seems to have made more impression upon him than the momentous political events which were then taking place. Nevertheless he and his companion Robert Jones could not help but be influenced by the mood of euphoria sweeping the country. The day after their arrival in France the King swore allegiance to the new constitution, and later they joined in celebrations to mark the first anniversary of the fall of the Bastille. The French Revolution was in its infancy and, as Wordsworth recalled in 'The Prelude', it aroused expectations of a glorious future:

> But 'twas a time when Europe was rejoiced,
> France standing on the top of golden hours,
> And human nature seeming born again.

Book VI, ll. 352–4

It was during his second visit to France (between November 1791 and December 1792) that he became seriously committed to the republican cause. He spent his time in Paris (where he visited the newly elected Legislative Assembly), Blois and Orléans. His political opinions were profoundly influenced by his friendship with Michel Beaupuy, an army officer he met in Blois. Beaupuy reinforced Wordsworth's conviction that the revolution was just, and he became an ardent supporter of the fight against poverty and inequality:

> And when we chanc'd
> One day to meet a hunger-bitten Girl,
> Who crept along, fitting her languid self
> Unto a Heifer's motion, by a cord
> Tied to her arm, and picking thus from the lane
> Its sustenance, while the Girl with her two hands
> Was busy knitting, in a heartless mood
> Of solitude, and at the sight my Friend
> In agitation said, ''Tis against that
> Which we are fighting,' I with him believed
> Devoutly that a spirit was abroad
> Which could not be withstood.

'The Prelude', Book IX, ll. 511–22

Wordsworth records in 'The Prelude' that he had become 'a Patriot' – that is, a republican:

> my heart was all
> Given to the People, and my love was theirs.

Book IX, ll. 125–6

He supported the moderate Girondins rather than the Jacobins (led by Robespierre). By the end of 1792 France had become a republic, Louis XVI was on trial (he was to be executed the following year) and the Girondins were losing the battle for control with the Jacobins. Wordsworth considered becoming an active revolutionary but in the event returned to England (according to 'The Prelude', 'Compell'd by nothing less than absolute want/ Of funds').

It was during this year in France that Wordsworth had a love affair with Annette Vallon, who gave birth to his daughter Caroline in December 1792. Very little is known about this relationship, the existence of which was not discovered until 1916 (during Wordsworth's lifetime knowledge of it had been confined to his family and a few intimate friends). He makes no direct reference to the affair in his poetry, though the tale of Vaudracour and Julia in Book IX of the 1805 'Prelude' gives a fictionalized account of the episode. When he left France he seems to have anticipated returning at a later date to marry Annette, and the reasons for this intention remaining unfulfilled are unknown. There were certainly a number of practical difficulties: he and Annette were of different religious beliefs; Wordsworth was a republican whereas Annette's family were strong royalists; and within a few months of his return to England from France the two countries were at war. He maintained contact with his former lover, however, paying for Caroline's education and later arranging for Annette herself to receive an allowance. Before his marriage to Mary Hutchinson in 1802 he went with Dorothy to visit Annette in Calais. Wordsworth's attitude to the episode, and the effect it had upon his poetry, can only be speculated upon, but the large number of abandoned women in his poems (Margaret in 'The Ruined Cottage' and the Forsaken Indian Woman are just two examples) suggests that he was sensitive to Annette's predicament and perhaps troubled by a sense of guilt.

After his arrival back in England, his identification with the revolution came under severe strain. In February 1793 Britain declared war on France. The resulting conflict of loyalties caused Wordsworth real anguish:

> *I felt*
> *The ravage of this most unnatural strife*
> *In my own heart; there lay it like a weight*
> *At enmity with all the tenderest springs*
> *Of my enjoyments.*

Book X, ll. 249–53

Believing that England had become the enemy of progress, he felt 'cut off' from his 'beloved Country', 'toss'd about in whirlwinds'. Another passage in 'The Prelude' describes attending a church service where prayers were said for British victories; he alone 'sate silent', feeling like 'an uninvited Guest'. A second source of anxiety was the growing violence in France. The Girondins fell from power and large numbers of them were executed by the Jacobins during the Reign of Terror. This 'domestic carnage' caused Wordsworth acute distress, and he began to feel that the principles of the revolution were being betrayed:

> *Through months, through years, long after the last beat*
> *Of those atrocities (I speak bare truth,*
> *As if to thee above in private talk)*
> *I scarcely had one night of quiet sleep*
> *Such ghastly visions had I of despair*
> *And tyranny, and implements of death,*
> *And long orations which in dreams I pleaded*
> *Before unjust Tribunals, with a voice*
> *Labouring, a brain confounded, and a sense,*
> *Of treachery and desertion in the place*
> *The holiest that I knew of, my own soul.*

Book X, ll. 370–80

His hopes revived when Robespierre was executed in July 1794, only to be dashed again by France's increasingly aggressive foreign policy:

> *And now become oppressors in their turn,*
> *Frenchmen had changed a war of self-defence*
> *For one of conquest, losing sight of all*
> *Which they had struggled for . . .*

Book X, ll. 791–4

By 1795 his support for France was at an end, though he stood by his approval of the revolution's early years. Accused in 1821 of having betrayed France, he asserted: 'You have been deluded by places and persons, while I have stuck to principles. I abandoned France and her rulers when they abandoned Liberty, gave themselves up to tyranny, and endeavoured to enslave the world.'

Disillusioned with the course of the revolution but still a political radical, Wordsworth sought solace in the philosophy of William Godwin. He had read Godwin's *Political Justice* (published in 1793) and when he met the philosopher in 1795 he became an ardent follower. Godwin was, like Wordsworth, a believer in justice and equality and an opponent of violence and war. He argued that humanity was naturally good and that the perfect society could be achieved only if all restraints upon people were removed; he therefore called for the abolition of all law and government. Reason, the supreme human faculty, should determine all aspects of our behaviour. Rather than allow ourselves to be swayed by emotion, we should, aiming always at what is to the general good, weigh up the advantages and disadvantages of different courses of action and arrive at logical and dispassionate conclusions. Wordsworth's emotional commitment to the French Revolution (not to mention his involvement with Annette Vallon) had left him bewildered and distressed, and the clarity and certainty of Godwin's faith in the rational intellect had obvious appeal.

Nevertheless, the repudiation of emotion went against Wordsworth's natural instincts and was unlikely to last. He soon realized that abstract reasoning did not provide an adequate answer to all moral problems. After a period of 'Dragging all passions, notions, shapes of faith' to the bar of reason, he eventually

> *lost*
> *All feeling of conviction, and, in fine,*
> *Sick, wearied out with contrarieties,*
> *Yielded up moral questions in despair.*

'The Prelude', Book X, ll. 897–900

'The Borderers', a verse tragedy probably written in 1796 and early 1797, demonstrates that evil can result if human nature is governed by intellectual principles alone. In a later note to the play Wordsworth explained that he was thinking particularly of the way in which the pursuance of the fine ideals of the French Revolution had had horrific consequences:

The study of human nature suggests this awful truth, that, as in the trials to which life subjects us, sin and crime are apt to start from their very opposite qualities, so are there no limits to the hardening of the heart, and the perversion of the understanding to which they may carry their slaves. During my long residence in France, while the Revolution was rapidly advancing to its extreme of wickedness, I had frequent opportunities of being an eye-witness of this process.

Godwinianism had increased rather than lessened Wordsworth's despair, but relief was to come from another source. In January 1795 he received a legacy of £900 from his friend Raisley Calvert, and this enabled him in September to set up house with his sister Dorothy at Racedown in Dorset. Since the family had been broken up they had met only at irregular intervals, but now Dorothy's presence revived memories of his childhood, and country walks with her reawakened his love of nature. In 'The Prelude' he pays tribute to the 'beloved Woman' who 'Maintain'd for me a saving intercourse/ With my true self'. Dorothy herself was remarkably sensitive to the natural world; the observations of nature contained in her Journals are strikingly vivid and evocative. Many of these observations found their way into Wordsworth's poetry, and the freshness and clarity of her perception undoubtedly influenced him (he said of her, 'She gave me eyes, she gave me ears').

Wordsworth's recovery was further assisted by his friendship with critic, philosopher and fellow-poet Samuel Taylor Coleridge. The two first met in Bristol in 1795 and stayed in contact over the next two years. Then, in July 1797, Wordsworth and Dorothy moved to Alfoxden in Somerset in order to be near Coleridge, who was living three miles away in Nether Stowey. Coleridge's encouragement increased Wordsworth's confidence in his own poetic gift. He also had a stimulating breadth of intellectual knowledge and showed Wordsworth that there were philosophical alternatives to Godwin. In particular, he deepened Wordsworth's interest in the ideas of David Hartley (1705–57). These were a development of previous theories of associationism. According to Hartley sense-impressions are the origin of all our thoughts, emotions and moral principles. Physical sensations (whether of pleasure or of pain) work on the consciousness and give rise to ideas which remain when the objects which caused them are no longer present. Our moral nature is therefore shaped by our environment. Although Wordsworth and Coleridge both later discarded some of Hartley's ideas and embraced other philosophical theories, the doctrine of associationism is central to much of Wordsworth's poetry and is particularly evident in the emphasis in 'The Prelude' on the influence of natural surroundings upon moral and spiritual growth.

The twelve months from July 1797 were a period of intense literary collaboration. Coleridge later commented that he, Wordsworth and Dorothy were 'Three persons and one soul'. Protracted discussions on the nature of poetry, long walking tours of the West Country and much reading of each other's work gave rise to numerous poems and laid the foundations for the critical theories advanced by Wordsworth in the Prefaces to the *Lyrical Ballads* and, much later, by Coleridge in *Biographia Literaria*. Most of Coleridge's best-known poems were written at this time, including 'Christabel', 'Kubla Khan' and 'The Ancient Mariner' (for which Wordsworth suggested the shooting of the albatross and the subsequent persecution of the mariner). Wordsworth wrote all the poems by him (except for 'Tintern Abbey') that appear in the first volume of *Lyrical Ballads*. The idea of working together on a book of poems originated on one of Wordsworth's and Coleridge's walking tours. They planned to cover their expenses by writing a poem for the *New Monthly Magazine*; that poem was to be 'The Ancient Mariner'. Wordsworth quickly realized however that his imagination was unsuited to the composition of poetry with a supernatural setting, and it was agreed that the writing of 'The Ancient Mariner' would be left to Coleridge. Instead, they would collaborate on a joint volume; there was to be a clear distinction between the types of poem the two of them would contribute, as Coleridge recalled in *Biographia Literaria*:

it was agreed that my endeavours should be directed to persons and characters supernatural, or at least romantic; yet so as to transfer from our inward nature a human interest and a semblance of truth sufficient to procure for these shadows of imagination that willing suspension of disbelief for the moment that constitutes poetic faith. Mr Wordsworth, on the other hand, was to propose to himself as his object to give the charm of novelty to the things of every day, and to excite a feeling analogous to the supernatural by awakening the mind's attention from the lethargy of custom and directing it to the loveliness and the wonder of the world before us.

In the event Coleridge contributed only four of the twenty-three poems in the book, though 'The Ancient Mariner' was given additional prominence by being placed at the front of the volume. Wordsworth's Preface to the second edition further clarifies his intentions. His object was 'to make the incidents of common life interesting by tracing in them, truly though not ostentatiously, the primary laws of our nature'. His subject-matter was to be drawn from 'low and rustic life' because in such a setting the 'essential passions of the heart' are more clearly exhibited. (In the poems themselves this interest in the simple and the primitive is also evident in the recurrence of figures who are in some way outside organized society: solitaries, children, the deranged.) In addition, there would be a deliberate rejection of conventional poetic diction in favour of 'the real language of men'.

The first volume is not consistent in its application of these principles, and the second departs even further from them, but several of the poems do conform broadly to Wordsworth's stated objectives. There are a number of rural ballads and narratives, with characters drawn from the poorest classes of society. Research has shown that this subject-matter was not as revolutionary as is sometimes claimed; readers of late eighteenth-century magazine poetry would have been quite accustomed to poems about abandoned women, bereaved mothers, convicts, beggars and peasants. A poem such as 'The Idiot Boy', which unembarrassedly celebrates the unique insights of a mentally defective child, was more daring and aroused some controversy. In some of the poems ('The Idiot Boy' and 'The Thorn', for example) the desire to avoid the 'gaudy and inane phraseology of many modern writers' takes the form of a deliberate triviality of expression, an attempt to emulate the language of ordinary speech:

> *There was a thorn; it looks so old*
> *In truth you'd find it hard to say,*
> *How it could ever have been young,*
> *It looks so old and grey.*

In other poems the language is less conversational but still has refreshing directness and simplicity when set against the elaborate diction of conventional eighteenth-century verse (and of Wordsworth's own early poetry). The greatest poems of his later years retain these qualities, but Wordsworth abandoned the use of colloquial language – probably wisely, for in the *Lyrical Ballads* it results too often in a dissipation of poetic intensity.

The first volume of *Lyrical Ballads*, published in September 1798, contains one poem markedly different from anything else in the book. 'Tintern Abbey' was added at the last moment, when the rest of the volume was already set up in type. In July 1798 Wordsworth and Dorothy visited Tintern while on their way to Bristol to oversee the

21

printing of *Lyrical Ballads*. Wordsworth later described how the poem came to be written:

> No poem of mine was composed under circumstances more pleasant for me to remember than this. I began it upon leaving Tintern, after crossing the Wye, and concluded it just as I was entering Bristol in the evening, after a ramble of four or five days, with my sister. Not a line of it was altered, and not any part of it written down till I reached Bristol.

The poem's elevated, meditative tone is in sharp contrast to the deliberate 'low' style of the ballads. Moreover, the content of the poem is deeply personal – a reflection upon the importance of nature to the poet and the way in which his relationship with nature has changed since boyhood. The autobiographical intensity of 'Tintern Abbey' indicates the course Wordsworth's poetic development was to take. The second volume of *Lyrical Ballads*, dated 1800 but published in January 1801, consisted entirely of poems by Wordsworth. The most notable of these are 'Michael', 'The Old Cumberland Beggar' and the remarkable Lucy poems – a group of beautiful lyrics about a dead girl.

In September 1798, just before the publication of *Lyrical Ballads*, Wordsworth travelled to Germany with Dorothy and Coleridge. After visiting Hamburg together, Coleridge went to Göttingen University while the Wordsworths travelled on to Goslar, a small northern town. There they passed a lonely winter, enduring the coldest weather of the century. Nevertheless, during these months Wordsworth wrote some of his greatest poetry, including most of the Lucy poems and parts of what were to become the first two 'books' of 'The Prelude'. The stay in Germany seems to have accelerated the increasing introspection of his verse; forced to look into himself for inspiration, he remembered with new understanding and appreciation experiences of his childhood and youth. It also reawakened his love for England, as is clear from the last of the Lucy poems, written two years later:

> *I travelled among unknown men,*
> *In lands beyond the sea;*
> *Nor, England! did I know till then*
> *What love I bore to thee.*

'The Prelude' was originally intended as an introduction to a long philosophical poem (to be called 'The Recluse') which would give Wordsworth's views on 'Man, Nature and Society'. Coleridge had encouraged him to compose such a work, and on 6 March 1798 Wordsworth wrote to a friend, James Tobin: 'I have written 1,300 lines of a poem in which I contrive to convey most of the knowledge of which I am possessed.' Some of this material was later incorporated into 'The Prelude'. Before he could begin 'The Recluse' Wordsworth felt he needed to prepare for the task ahead by examining his own growth as a poet. He therefore planned an autobiographical poem, to be addressed to Coleridge. Two books were completed by 1800; Wordsworth then thought of extending it to five books, but by the time the whole poem was finished in 1805 it had grown to thirteen books. The middle section of 'The Recluse' was published as 'The Excursion' in 1814; the other two parts were never completed. 'The Prelude: or, Growth of a Poet's Mind' was not published until after Wordsworth's death. A poem of such length on the development of an individual was, as Wordsworth knew, something completely new. 'It is a thing unprecedented in literary history,' he observed, 'that a man should talk so much about himself.' The poem begins in childhood and explores, in verse of wonderful vividness and immediacy and acute psychological insight, his earliest experiences of nature. Later books cover such topics as his schooldays, Cambridge, his walking tour of the Alps, residence in London and the impact upon him of the French Revolution. It should not however be read as a strictly chronological autobiography; as its full title indicates, the poem is an account of *inner* growth rather than a mere recital of important events, and this gives rise to passages of reflection and occasional movements backwards or forwards in time. A recurring theme is Wordsworth's sense of himself as a poet, and his consequent obligation to fulfil his creative potential.

After its completion Wordsworth continued to revise the poem throughout his life. The final version was published in 1850, but it was not until 1926 that the original 1805 text, edited from manuscripts by Professor Ernest de Selincourt, appeared. The later version contains some improvements in style, strengthening the continuity of the poem, correcting errors of syntax and in places enhancing the verse's clarity. However, many of the alterations reflect a depressing decline in poetic power. As de Selincourt comments, 'In the years when his inspiration was flagging, Wordsworth tended to fall back on that same abstract and artificial language from which his own theories, and his own best practice, had been a reaction.' De Selincourt illustrates his point by comparing a number of passages from the two texts. In the 1805 version, for example, the meeting with the discharged soldier in Book IV is introduced by the following:

> *A favourite pleasure hath it been with me,*
> *From time of earliest youth, to walk alone*
> *Along the public Way, when, for the night*

> *Deserted, in its silence it assumes*
> *A character of deeper quietness*
> *Than pathless solitudes.*

Book IV, ll. 363–8

In the 1850 text we find a more consciously literary passage, the grandiloquence of which is much less evocative than the bare simplicity of the original version:

> *When from our better selves we have too long*
> *Been parted by the hurrying world, and drop.*
> *Sick of its business, of its pleasure tired,*
> *How gracious, how benign is Solitude!*

The changes in the 1850 text also reflect shifts in Wordsworth's political, philosophical and religious attitudes. Here again there is more loss than gain, the orthodox opinions of his middle and later years displacing the radicalism and unconventionality of his youth. His support for the French Revolution is toned down and, in order to conform to conventional Christian principles, rapturous descriptions of intense personal communion with nature are altered so that there is less suggestion of human self-sufficiency. Thus the following from the 1805 text:

> *I worshipp'd then among the depths of things*
> *As my soul bade me; could I then take part*
> *In aught but admiration, or be pleased*
> *With anything but humbleness and love;*
> *I felt, and nothing else . . .*

Book XI, ll. 234–8

becomes in the 1850 version:

> *Worshipping then among the depth of things,*
> *As piety ordained; could I submit*
> *To measured admiration, or to aught*
> *That should preclude humility and love?*
> *I felt, observed, and pondered.*

For all its occasional infelicities the 1805 'Prelude' has a vigour and an immediacy that are too often lacking in the later version, and it certainly strikes the reader as more faithful to the realities of Wordsworth's early years.

Soon after his return to England from Germany in 1799 Wordsworth and Dorothy set up home at Dove Cottage in Grasmere, where they were to remain for eight years. The decision to live once more in the Lake District was no doubt motivated by memories of the idyllic relationship with nature he had enjoyed in childhood. It also suggests a desire for calm and stability after the restless wanderings and emotional upheavals of youth. That he was looking for a more settled existence is confirmed by his marriage to Mary Hutchinson (a childhood friend) in October 1802. As well as concluding the first version of 'The Prelude' Wordsworth wrote during these years a great number of shorter poems, including several of those for which he is most remembered: 'The Solitary Reaper', 'I wandered lonely as a cloud', 'Michael' and the Immortality Ode. For some of this time he was again stimulated by the company of Coleridge, who came to live in nearby Keswick in July 1800. Coleridge's influence on the Prefaces Wordsworth included in the 1800 and 1802 editions of *Lyrical Ballads* was such that he later claimed, 'The Preface is half a child of my own brain.'

By now, however, Coleridge's mental and physical health was seriously deteriorating. His marriage was unhappy and he had fallen in love with Sara Hutchinson, Wordsworth's sister-in-law – a hopeless passion which brought him only despair. He was becoming increasingly addicted to the opium he took to combat gout and other ailments. In 1804 he left for Malta in an attempt to salvage his health and overcome his emotional difficulties; the period of collaboration with Wordsworth was effectively at an end. When he returned in 1806 the Wordsworths were shocked by the change in him: he was lethargic and overweight and his dependence on opium was clearly affecting his personality. Although he came to live with the Wordsworths in 1808 (they had now moved to another house in Grasmere, Allan Bank), the relationship between the two poets was under increasing strain. The final quarrel occurred in 1810. Coleridge travelled to London with a mutual acquaintance who repeated to him some remarks Wordsworth had passed on Coleridge's personal habits. He was said to have described Coleridge as 'an absolute nuisance' who had 'rotted his entrails out by intemperance'. Coleridge took violent offence at this and when he passed through Grasmere in 1812 did not call at the Wordsworths' house. Later that year a reconciliation of sorts did take place, but the old intimacy would never be restored. Coleridge wrote in a letter: 'All outward actions, all inward wishes, all thoughts and admirations will be the same – are the same, but – aye, there remains an immedicable *But*.'

In addition to the rift with Coleridge, there were other events which overshadowed Wordsworth's middle years and had a profound effect on his outlook on life and, inevitably, on his poetry. The opening stanzas of the Immortality Ode, composed in 1802, lament the loss of the visionary power of youth. Earlier poems had celebrated his ability to sense, during moments of unusually heightened awareness, an invisible life in and beyond nature. This ability had now deserted him: 'The things which I have seen I now can see no more.' Although the later stanzas of the poem assert the consolation to be gained from remembering the visionary insights of earlier years, a vital source of inspiration had nevertheless been lost. A second shattering blow was the death of his brother John, who drowned at sea in 1805. He sought relief from emotional distress in a hard stoicism. 'Elegiac Stanzas Suggested by a Picture of Peele Castle', written in 1806, praises the castle as an example of strength and durability in the face of adversity:

> *And this huge Castle, standing here sublime,*
> *I love to see the look with which it braves,*
> *Cased in the unfeeling armour of old time,*
> *The lightning, the fierce wind, and trampling waves.*

Wordsworth appears to have felt that stability could be achieved only if a rigid control was imposed on his emotional life. The 'Ode to Duty' (written between 1804 and 1806) expresses his weariness of 'unchartered freedom' and longing for 'a repose that ever is the same'. The free-thinking of his earlier years was curbed in favour of a more orthodox Christianity.

Politically, his endorsement of conventional attitudes took the form of an increasing conservatism. He deliberately sought the patronage of Sir William Lowther, the Earl of Lonsdale; the Lowthers were the most powerful aristocratic family in Cumberland and Westmorland and Sir William was a distant relation of the Lord Lonsdale who had employed Wordsworth's father. In 1813, after he had requested the Earl's assistance in obtaining a position which was lucrative but not too onerous, Wordsworth was appointed Distributor of Stamps for Westmorland, a post which brought him about £300 a year. He repaid his debt by assisting the Lowthers in parliamentary elections. Two sons of the Earl were Tory Members of Parliament for Westmorland, occupying seats which the Lowther family had held unopposed for forty-four years. In the general election of 1818, however, they faced opposition from a Whig candidate, Henry Brougham. Wordsworth acted as a kind of undercover agent for the Lowthers, sending them reports on political meetings and advising them of the voting intentions of local citizens. He also assisted in the dubious practice of buying land with Lowther money, then dividing it up and selling the lots to known Tory supporters, who as freeholders would now be able to vote in the election. In an anonymous pamphlet, *Address to the Freeholders of Westmorland*, Wordsworth argued against the parliamentary reforms advocated by Brougham and in favour of restricting the franchise to property-owners. He was by this time a substantial man of property himself. He had accepted a small estate at Applethwaite, near Keswick, from Sir George Beaumont and with the help of £200 from the Earl of Lonsdale had purchased another property for £1,000 at Ullswater. His views on parliamentary suffrage had certainly undergone a pronounced change since 1793, when he had declared in his letter to the Bishop of Llandaff: 'If there is a single man in Great Britain who has no suffrage in the election of a representative, the will of the society of which he is a member is not generally expressed; he is a Helot in that society.'

Wordsworth's behaviour provoked Shelley to comment: 'What a beastly and pitiful wretch that Wordsworth! That such a man should be such a poet! I can compare him with no one but Simonides, the flatterer of the Sicilian tyrants, and at the same time the most natural and tender of lyric poets.' Keats shared Shelley's disappointment ('Wordsworth versus Brougham! Sad – sad – sad!') but in subsequent elections Wordsworth again gave his support to the Lowthers. In 1842 he gave up his Distributorship of Stamps but arranged for it to be transferred to his son William. The financial loss that this entailed was soon offset by the provision of a civil-list pension of £300 a year.

It is difficult not to perceive a strong element of pecuniary self-interest in Wordsworth's later political attitudes, but his commitment to order and stability seems also to have answered an urgent emotional need. In repressing his inner life, however, he stifled the source of his poetry. The dramatic decline in the quality of his verse after 1805 is well known. Up until his death in 1850 he continued to write prolifically but the work of these years is for the most part depressingly flat and passionless. His great philosophical poem 'The Recluse' remained unwritten except for the section known as 'The Excursion' and a fragment of 800 lines published posthumously as 'Home at Grasmere'. Instead he returned again and again to 'The Prelude'; altogether there are seventeen major 'Prelude' manuscripts in the Wordsworth Library in Grasmere. His genius was not suited to generalized reflections upon human nature; it was the urge to explore his own life that gave rise to his greatest poetry, and this was never entirely suppressed.

2. *Lyrical Ballads*

The previous chapter described how the two volumes of *Lyrical Ballads* originated and discussed Wordsworth and Coleridge's intentions when they collaborated on the first edition of 1798. This chapter and the next will be given over to a detailed analysis of some of the more significant poems.

'Simon Lee' and 'The Idiot Boy'

These two poems are amongst those corresponding most closely to Wordsworth's own description of the *Lyrical Ballads* in the Preface of 1800. They relate simple incidents drawn from 'low and rustic life' and employ language close to everyday speech. Simon Lee is an 'Old Huntsman' (as the full title of the poem indicates) and is encountered by the narrator as he is attempting to dig out the root of an old tree. The apparent triviality of the poem's content is matched by the triteness of its language, and the poem has been judged a failure by many critics. The poem's artlessness was clearly deliberate, however, and we should not dismiss the finished product as unworthy of serious attention before making an attempt to establish what lay behind Wordsworth's choice of approach and subject-matter.

The first eight stanzas of the poem detail Simon Lee's old age, poverty and ill health, and contrast his present frailties with the accomplishments of his youth, when, a vigorous and expert huntsman, 'He all the country could outrun,/ Could leave both men and horse behind.' Now, following the deaths of his master and his hunting companions, he and his wife live alone and childless. The livery he wears and the now deserted 'Hall of Ivor' are pathetic reminders of past glories. The facts of Simon's decline are recounted in a tone of detached, ironic observation, and at this stage in the poem the reader is not likely to feel much sympathetic involvement in his plight. In several places the jaunty rhythm, trite rhymes and banal content combine to suggest that *mirth* might actually be the most appropriate response:

> *Of years he has upon his back*
> *No doubt, a burthen weighty;*
> *He says he is three score and ten,*
> *But others say he's eighty.*

(In an apparent attempt to dignify the language of the poem, these lines were omitted from later versions.) As the poem continues in this vein the reader's puzzlement increases; is this work as slight as it appears or is something more serious, more substantial, about to be revealed to us? The poem does contain such a development, but it takes an unexpected form. The turning-point comes in the ninth stanza when we discover that Wordsworth is indeed conscious of his reader's likely reaction to the poem's content so far:

> *My gentle reader, I perceive*
> *How patiently you've waited,*
> *And now I fear that you expect*
> *Some tale will be related.*

The mode of expression is as unsophisticated as before, but the narrator is at least aware of the inconsequentiality of much of the early part of the poem and that this has tested the reader's patience.

The last two lines quoted above, however, indicate that any hope that there will now be a dramatic twist to Simon Lee's story will be disappointed. And what follows is, on the face of it, as commonplace as before. The narrator tells how one summer's day he came across Simon struggling to uproot an old tree stump, took his axe from him and severed the tangled root with one blow. Nevertheless, Wordsworth achieves in this conclusion genuine pathos and profundity – an achievement which takes us by surprise and prompts us to reassess the entire poem. This unexpected emotional depth is disclosed in the final stanza:

> *The tears into his eyes were brought,*
> *And thanks and praises seemed to run*
> *So fast out of his heart, I thought*
> *They never would have done.*
> *– I've heard of hearts unkind, kind deeds*
> *With coldness still returning.*
> *Alas! the gratitude of men*
> *Has oftener left me mourning.*

Suddenly our sympathies are engaged and, like that narrator, we are no longer observing with detachment the misfortunes of an insignificant, rather comical old man. The episode, like many others described in his poems, illustrates Wordsworth's belief that commonplace incidents can produce moments of insight into universal truths of human experience, into what he called in the 1800 Preface 'the great and simple affections of our nature'. Simon's tears, and the poet's 'mourning', are partly caused by the tragedy of old age. The contrast between age and youth in the earlier account of Simon's life has been dramatized in the encounter between a strong and healthy narrator and a feeble old man trying vainly to remove a tree stump. But as well as weeping for what he has lost Simon weeps for what he has received – for the kindness shown to him by the poet, who in turn is moved by his gratitude and led to reflect sadly that such fellow-feeling is too often absent from human relationships. The poem emphasizes the importance of such values as gratitude, generosity and mutual respect.

The earlier part of the poem now takes on a new significance. The very ordinariness of Simon Lee's age, poverty and generally enfeebled condition is what is important. The poem shows how easy it is to take a detached, dismissive view of this man's tragedy before shocking us into the realization that what has been described really *is* a tragedy, a universal human tragedy of which we are the victims as much as Simon Lee. Whether the poem as a whole succeeds however is very much a matter for personal judgement. Critics are divided between those who argue that the beginning of the poem is redeemed – and justified – by the conclusion and those who believe that the effectiveness of this conclusion is fatally undermined by what precedes it. The intensity of disagreement demonstrates how fraught with difficulty was the task Wordsworth set himself in *Lyrical Ballads*.

A similar division of opinion exists concerning 'The Idiot Boy', a poem which runs similar risks. Again the poem has a humble rural setting and describes a simple incident. A mother, Betty Foy, sends her retarded son Johnny to fetch the doctor for a sick neighbour and when the child does not return has to scour the countryside before finding him safe and taking him home. As in 'Simon Lee', the episode is used to illustrate certain 'essential passions of the heart', in particular the love shown to Johnny by his mother and their neighbour Susan Gale, and Johnny's own peculiar innocence. The poem's narrator relates his tale in plain, colloquial language ('What means this bustle, Betty Foy?/ Why are you in this mighty fret?' – ll. 8–9), and this approach has again exasperated several critics. Graham Hough, for example, argues that 'a real imaginative intuition about the strangeness and incommunicability of the poor crazy child's moonlight adventures seems to be struggling in a waste of garrulity and trivial expression'. In its language and form (the poem is divided into strongly rhymed stanzas and moves along at a rapid pace) 'The Idiot Boy' is in the tradition of popular comic ballads. Wordsworth's choice of subject-matter, however, was unusual and gave rise to a certain amount of controversy. Among those who were offended by Wordsworth's treatment of his central character was Coleridge, who expressed sympathy with the view that

the author has not, in the poem itself, taken sufficient care to preclude from the reader's fancy the disgusting images of ordinary, morbid idiocy, which yet it was by no means his intention to represent. He has even by the 'burr, burr, burr,' uncounteracted by any preceding description of the boy's beauty, assisted in recalling them.

Biographia Literaria, Chapter XVIII

Many readers may well feel that it is the very absence of sentimentality which is one of the poem's strengths. Johnny is portrayed truthfully and with respect for his individuality; indeed, his joyful openness to the world about him leads Wordsworth to see him as the possessor of a wisdom denied to others.

The narrative voice of the poem is that of a humble rustic who has a ready understanding of Betty Foy's feelings, who recounts the story in her language and comments on her actions in a familiar, neighbourly tone:

> *There's none to help poor Susan Gale;*
> *What must be done? What will betide?*

ll. 30–31

At the same time the narrator does not identify completely with his characters, and we sense his amusement at some of Betty's sillier moments, as when she goes to the doctor in search of Johnny and forgets to tell him of Susan Gale's illness. The poem is never contemptuous of Betty, however, and the strength of her love for Johnny is clearly valued. It is seen first in her rash decision to send him to the doctor; she wishes to give Johnny a sense of pride and achievement by entrusting him with an important errand. Her devotion is then demonstrated by her increasing fear for Johnny's safety when he does not return, her frantic search for him and her immense relief when he is found. Betty's humanity is further expressed in her kind-hearted concern for the well-being of her neighbours. Susan Gale herself has a similar unselfish anxiety for both Betty and Johnny, and is rewarded by a miraculous recovery:

> *Long time lay Susan lost in thought,*
> *And many dreadful fears beset her,*
> *Both for her Messenger and Nurse;*
> *And, as her mind grew worse and worse,*
> *Her body it grew better.*

ll. 412–16

Betty, Johnny and Susan Gale are thus bound together by warmth and compassion, by feelings of human sympathy that are given additional emphasis by the contrasting coldness and indifference of the doctor. Betty's selfless love of her son is of course the most important element in this network of caring relationships, and the extent to which Wordsworth intended us to be impressed by it is indicated by a letter he wrote on the poem in 1802: 'I have indeed often looked upon the conduct of fathers and mothers of the lower classes of society towards idiots as the great triumph of the human heart. It is there that we see the strength, disinterestedness and grandeur of love.'

Another remark in the same letter points us to the poem's other centre of interest: 'I have often applied to idiots, in my own mind, that sublime expression of Scripture, that *their life is hidden with God.*' In terms of 'The Idiot Boy' this seems to mean that Johnny has a peculiarly close, intuitive relationship with the natural world, a relationship unattainable by the more 'intelligent'. Johnny is in permanent, effortless possession of the tranquillity and joy which derive from a feeling of complete accord with nature and to which Wordsworth himself had access only during *moments* of visionary experience:

> *For joy he cannot hold the bridle,*
> *For joy his head and heels are idle,*
> *He's idle all for very joy.*
>
> *And while the pony moves his legs,*
> *In Johnny's left-hand you may see*
> *The green bough's motionless and dead:*
> *The Moon that shines above his head*
> *Is not more still and mute than he.*

ll.74–81

As Johnny contentedly continues his journey, this oneness with the world of nature is continually emphasized; he babbles to the accompaniment of hooting owls and there are repeated references to the moon overhead.

The narrative then concentrates on Betty's worried reaction to his disappearance, but when Johnny re-enters the poem he is found to be unharmed and still at ease with nature:

> *Who's you, that, near the waterfall,*
> *Which thunders down with headlong force,*
> *Beneath the moon, yet shining fair,*

> *As careless as if nothing were,*
> *Sits upright on a feeding horse . . .*

ll. 347–51

The narrator seems unnerved by the thunderous waterfall (it is also a source of worry to Betty Foy), but Johnny happily accepts it as part of the natural scene, completely oblivious to its danger. The boy's unique perception of life is captured in his own description of his adventure at the close of the poem:

> *'The cocks did crow to-whoo, to-whoo,*
> *And the sun did shine so cold!'*
> *– Thus answered Johnny in his glory,*
> *And that was all his travel's story.*

ll. 450–53

The word 'glory' indicates that Johnny's irrational account is not to be laughingly dismissed. It is precisely his lack of a rational, ordering intelligence which makes possible his unthinking, joyful immersion in the sights and sounds of nature.

'The Last of the Flock', 'The Female Vagrant' and 'The Old Cumberland Beggar'

As was noted in the previous chapter, many of the *Lyrical Ballads* portray characters outside the mainstream of society – the poor, the deranged, the rejected. In describing the plight of these figures the poems are often a vehicle for the expression of radical social and political views. 'The Last of the Flock', for example, draws attention to iniquities in the application of the poor laws. The system of parish relief was such that a man with any amount of property could not receive assistance. This meant that the small independent farmer in need of temporary relief had to sell all his property before he was eligible for it, thereby destroying his livelihood and his chances of recovery. In 'The Last of the Flock' the narrator meets a farmer in exactly this predicament; trapped in a downward spiral of poverty, he has had to sell off his sheep one by one. The parish has refused him assistance on the grounds that he is a 'wealthy man'. The poem is also an attack upon the Godwinian notion that ownership of property is the root of evil. The shepherd's flock is a source of pride to him and strengthens his love for the family it enables him to provide for; its eradication is accompanied by an erosion of his dignity and a degenerating relationship with his children. (Wordsworth's

33

admiration of the small private farmer is also evident in 'Michael', discussed in the next chapter.)

'The Female Vagrant', in its original version at least, condemns the callousness of wealthy landowners, the evils of war and society's general oppression of the poor. The vagrant of the title narrates her own story, and tells how she and her father were forced from their home by an aggressive landowner. She married but again fell into poverty, then emigrated to America where her husband and children were killed by war and disease. Finally she returned to England alone and destitute. The poem was frequently revised, appearing as a single poem in various versions and also incorporated in a larger poem called originally 'Salisbury Plain' but later 'Guilt and Sorrow'. In the later versions the radical tone was softened, reflecting Wordsworth's increasing conservatism. In the 1798 edition of *Lyrical Ballads*, for example, the fifth and sixth stanzas describe the landowner's victimization of the narrator's father, but in the final version these are replaced by a more generalized apportioning of blame:

> *But through severe mischance and cruel wrong,*
> *My father's substance fell into decay.*

The pacifist element in the poem was similarly curtailed. The description of British soldiers as 'the brood/ That lap (their very nourishment) their brother's blood' disappears after the 1800 edition.

'The Old Cumberland Beggar' also has an explicit political message, but the poem's significance goes considerably beyond this. The central figure is one of Wordsworth's most memorable characters and belongs with the solitaries who feature so frequently in his poetry (other notable instances are 'Resolution and Independence' and several episodes in 'The Prelude'). Apart from their isolation the main link between these characters is that they are all in some way integrated with the natural world.

The opening description of the beggar expresses his loneliness by emphasizing the secluded nature of his surroundings:

> *Surrounded by those wild unpeopled hills,*
> *He sat, and ate his food in solitude.*

ll. 14–15

The poem goes on to describe him as 'a solitary Man' (ll. 24, 44) and 'this solitary being' (l. 110). Nevertheless, the beggar does have a relationship with both the natural landscape and the inhabitants of the 'Hamlets and thinly-scattered villages' he travels through, and the poem's main concern is to explore these relationships. As is often the case with Wordsworth's solitaries, he is so much a part of nature that his attributes seem more those of an inanimate object than of a human being. Although old there is about him a suggestion of the eternal; he appears to be unaffected by human time:

> Him from my childhood have I known; and then
> He was so old, he seems not older now . . .

ll. 22–3

His steady but barely perceptible movement is like that of some indiscernible natural process. He 'travels on' but

> he is so still
> In look and motion, that the cottage curs,
> Ere he have pass'd the door, will turn away,
> Weary of barking at him. Boys and girls,
> The vacant and the busy, maids and youths,
> And urchins newly-breeched – all pass him by:
> Him even the slow-paced waggon leaves behind.

ll. 60–66

He seems unconscious of other people, never speaking with those who give him alms and ignoring the warning shouts of the carriage-driver (ll. 37–43). He is unconscious of his natural surroundings also; he is bent double with age and his eyes gaze fixedly at the small patch of ground immediately before him. Even then, he is described as 'seeing still/ And seldom knowing that he sees' (ll. 53–4). But being deprived of the sight of 'fields with rural works, of hill and dale,/ And the blue sky' (ll. 49–50) paradoxically increases the old man's closeness to the elements of nature. He merges unthinkingly with his environment, rather than viewing it as a detached observer, conscious of his own independent existence.

The beggar is inevitably unaware of the profound influence he has upon others. Wherever he goes he acts as a stimulus to kindness and charity, causing people to exercise the 'simple affections of our nature' which were so important to Wordsworth. The horseman interrupts his journey to place a coin carefully in the old man's hat; the post-boy patiently steers his car around him. Such actions benefit the giver as well as the receiver; the poor housewife who gives the beggar a handful of grain returns from her door 'with exhilarated heart' (l. 160). He is a reminder to the villagers of past acts of charity, and this prompts them to further kindness: 'The mild necessity of use compels/ To acts of love' (ll. 99–100). Benevolence of this kind helps to shape the moral character, and the soul becomes

35

'insensibly disposed/ To virtue and true goodness' (ll. 104–5). The beggar, though in many respects isolated from his community, nevertheless enforces the recognition that 'we have all of us one human heart' (l. 153).

The old man thus has a valuable social function, and it is partly this that gives rise to the overt political content of the poem. Wordsworth condemns those 'Statesmen' (l. 67) who would judge the beggar a public nuisance and remove him to a workhouse. This attack on the utilitarian attitudes of politicians would itself be callous and insensitive if Wordsworth were simply arguing that beggars, regardless of their suffering, should be left untouched because they give people the opportunity to exercise charity. He certainly recognizes and values the old man's use to the community, but his view is also based upon genuine respect and sympathy for the old man himself. It would be wrong and unnatural to deny the beggar the care and spontaneous fellowship of others; it is 'Nature's law' that not even 'the meanest of created things'

> should exist
> *Divorced from good – a spirit and pulse of good,*
> *A life and soul, to every mode of being*
> *Inseparably linked.*

ll. 76–9

Moreover, it would also be wrong to destroy the old man's unique empathy with nature. Wordsworth recognizes the harshness of the beggar's existence, the 'frosty air' and 'winter snows' to which he is exposed (l. 174), but to wrench him from the environment he has chosen and to which he so palpably belongs would be crueller still:

> *As in the eye of Nature he has liv'd,*
> *So in the eye of Nature let him die.*

ll. 196–7

'Expostulation and Reply' and 'The Tables Turned'

These two poems are significant because they offer an explicit account of some of Wordsworth's central ideas about nature. Wordsworth explains in a note that the poems arose 'out of conversation with a friend who was somewhat unreasonably attached to modern books of moral philosophy'. The friend was William Hazlitt, though the person addressed in the poems (identified as 'Matthew' in 'Expostulation and Reply') is also based upon William Taylor, Wordsworth's Hawkshead schoolmaster.

In 'The Tables Turned' the poet reproaches his friend, urging him to abandon his books and enjoy the delights of nature. The poem should not be seen as an attack upon all reading but as a repudiation of the kind of reductive rationalism which regards the intellect as separate from, and superior to, the senses. If the intellect overpowers the senses, Wordsworth argues, it can destroy the spontaneous pleasure we derive from natural beauty:

> *Our meddling intellect*
> *Misshapes the beauteous form of things: –*
> *We murder to dissect.*

Again, nature is seen as a beneficent, educative influence: 'Let Nature be your Teacher' and 'Sweet is the love which Nature brings'.

'Nutting', 'There was a Boy' and 'We are Seven'

The autobiographical poems 'Nutting' and 'There was a Boy' provide graphic illustration of the influence of nature upon the growth of a child's consciousness. 'Nutting' recalls a boyhood expedition to gather hazelnuts. The buoyant opening superbly captures the boy's sense of adventure as he sallies forth equipped with wallet and nutting crook. He comes across a beautiful nook, hitherto undiscovered. Much of Wordsworth's best poetry recreates the experiences of a boy alone with nature. Here the privacy of the experience is emphasized by the isolated location; it is an 'unvisited spot' in a 'far-distant wood' (ll. 16, 17), and to reach it the boy has to force his way through vegetation and over 'pathless rocks' (l. 14). After a short period of gazing upon the scene and relaxedly enjoying its beauty the boy savagely attacks the trees, alliteration and heavy monosyllables emphasizing the sudden explosion of brutality:

> *Then up I rose,*
> *And dragged to earth both branch and bough, with crash*
> *And merciless ravage.*

> ll. 43–5

When he leaves the glade the boy is triumphant, 'rich beyond the wealth of kings' (l. 51), though the poet believes he also felt regret at what he had done.

In destroying the bower the boy shows an insensitivity to the life that is in nature, and that links nature to man. Immediately he entered the nook he was overtaken by a selfish longing to possess its beauty, crediting it with no other purpose than that of satisfying his sensual appetite; anticipating the fulfilment of his desire, he 'eyed/ The banquet' (ll. 24–5).

It is appropriate that the boy's violation of the peaceful woodland glade is compared to a rape. The nook is a 'virgin scene' which when mercilessly ravaged made no response but 'patiently gave up' its 'quiet being' and was left 'Deform'd and sullied' (ll. 21, 47–8). David Pirie makes the interesting observation that elsewhere in Wordsworth the ideal relationship between man and nature – a relationship in which there is genuine mutual interchange – is described in terms of a marriage. The Preface to the 1814 edition of 'The Excursion' speaks of 'the discerning intellect of Man' being 'wedded to this goodly universe' and of 'The spousal verse/ Of this great consummation'. The 'sense of pain' (l. 52) Wordsworth thinks he felt at the end of the nutting episode suggests that the boy learnt from his experience. It left him with a changed perception of nature: an increased awareness of nature's 'quiet being' and of the respect that this deserves.

'There was a Boy' recollects another solitary experience of nature. The boy of the poem would spend many of his evenings imitating the hooting of owls, in the hope that real owls would respond to his cries. In describing the resultant eruption of natural sounds Wordsworth vividly evokes the excitement and exuberance of the experience:

> and they would shout
> Across the watery vale and shout again,
> Responsive to his call, – with quivering peals,
> And long halloos, and screams, and echoes loud
> Redoubled and redoubled; concourse wild
> Of jocund din!

But the poem then duplicates the pattern of 'Nutting', where an outburst of physical activity was unexpectedly followed by a quieter sensation:

> And, when there came a pause
> Of silence such as baffled his best skill:
> Then, sometimes, in that silence, while he hung
> Listening, a gentle shock of mild surprise
> Has carried far into his heart the voice
> Of mountain-torrents; or the visible scene
> Would enter unawares into his mind
> With all its solemn imagery, its rocks,
> Its woods, and that uncertain heaven received
> Into the bosom of the steady lake.

The boy begins with an unsubtle, energetically physical relationship with the natural world (in 'Tintern Abbey' Wordsworth refers to the 'glad animal movements' of his childhood). There is interchange of a sort – the owls are 'Responsive to his call' – but the ensuing experience is clearly of deeper significance. In Wordsworth's poetry visionary insight is frequently associated with the suspension of activity, and here the feeling of suspension is finely captured in the line-division of 'hung/ Listening'. In the silence that follows his dialogue with the owls the boy experiences nature with a new kind of intensity and has an intuitive sense of his own connections with the external world; as the sights and sounds of nature pour into his heart and mind the boy and the torrents, rocks, woods and lake around him are – again the quotation is from 'Tintern Abbey' – 'interfus'd'. The notion of the ultimate harmony and tranquillity of the universe is brilliantly reinforced by the image of the sky entering 'Into the bosom of the steady lake' (Coleridge was greatly impressed by these lines and believed them to be immediately recognizable as Wordsworth's: 'had I met these lines running wild in the deserts of Arabia, I should have instantly screamed out "Wordsworth!"'.) The boy's unconsciousness of the full significance of his experience is important, and is indicated by 'unawares'; unknown to the child, the images of nature entering his mind would exercise a permanent influence on his perception of the world. Wordsworth later wrote of the poem: 'I have represented a commutation and transfer of internal feelings co-operating with external accidents to plant, for immortality, images of sound and sight in the celestial soil of the imagination' (Preface to *Poems*, 1815).

The concluding stanza, which tells us the boy died before he was ten years old, was added to the original manuscript version of the poem and has puzzled and disappointed many critics. It is felt that it weakens the overall effect of the poem, and Wordsworth has been accused of sentimentality and (by F. W. Bateson) of 'literary carpentry'. However, the knowledge that in the earliest version of the poem the boy was Wordsworth himself enables us to put an interesting construction on this final stanza, one which would strengthen its validity. If the character of the boy is based upon Wordsworth, the poet who stands strangely 'Mute' by his grave for 'A full half-hour' (ll. 30–1) is in a sense looking at his *own* grave – that is, reflecting upon the death of his boyhood self. The intuitive sense of the ultimate harmony of man and nature is at its most intense in childhood and inevitably diminishes with the passing of time (this is the theme of the Immortality Ode). At the close of the poem Wordsworth can therefore be seen as mourning the loss of the visionary power of his boyhood.

Childhood perception is also the subject of 'We are Seven'. The poem illustrates again Wordsworth's use of simple 'incidents of common life' to illuminate 'primary laws of our nature'. It is based upon a conversation the poet had with a little girl in the West Country in 1793. In the poem the adult narrator asks an eight-year-old 'cottage girl' how many brothers and sisters she has. She tells him she has seven, but it then becomes apparent to the narrator that two of them are dead. The adult repeatedly points out, 'Then ye are only five', but the child continues to insist, 'We are seven.' The language of the poem is plain and unsophisticated, and this, together with the simplicity of the content, has meant that it has often shared the fate of 'Simon Lee' and 'The Idiot Boy' and been dismissed as trivial nonsense. Wordsworth was certainly aware of the risk he was taking in publishing the poem; before the *Lyrical Ballads* went to press a friend, James Tobin (the 'dear brother Jim' of the opening stanza), urged him to omit it because it would make him 'everlastingly ridiculous'. Wordsworth replied, 'Nay, that shall take its chance, however.'

Essentially the content of the poem is *not* trivial. Wordsworth evidently regarded the ignorance of mortality as one of the central characteristics of childhood experience. In another context he recalled that 'Nothing was more difficult for me in childhood than to admit the notion of death as a state applicable to my own being.' As so often in Wordsworth the child's perception of reality is seen as superior to the adult's. There is an ironic emphasis on the contrast between the worldly sophistication of the narrator, evident in his patronizing tone at the beginning of the poem ('A simple child ... What should it know of death?'), and the rustic simplicity of the cottage girl, who has a 'woodland air' and is 'wildly clad' (ll. 9–10). The adult is capable of mathematical calculation but lacks the child's intuitive awareness of eternal nature. Interestingly it is the narrator who holds the conventional religious notion of life after death, telling the girl that her brother and sister are 'in Heaven' (l. 62). But to the child Heaven is an irrelevance; the living and the dead are inseparable. She has not lost her brother and sister but continues to enjoy with them a shared existence.

3. The Lucy Poems, 'Michael' and 'Tintern Abbey'

With the exception of one of the five Lucy poems, the poems examined in this chapter appeared in either the first or the second volume of *Lyrical Ballads*. They have been separated from the poems discussed in the previous chapter because of their importance and because, for reasons that will emerge in the course of our discussion of them, they are markedly different from most of the other *Lyrical Ballads*.

The Lucy Poems

Four of the Lucy poems were written in Germany (during William and Dorothy's stay there from October 1798 to April 1799) and published in the 1800 edition of *Lyrical Ballads*. The fifth, 'I travelled among unknown men', was probably written in 1801 and was first published in 1807. All five poems allude to the death, real or imagined, of a girl who in four of the poems is named 'Lucy'. There has been much speculation over the girl's identity. There is no evidence that at the time of writing the poems Wordsworth had loved a girl who died, and many commentators have been guided by Coleridge's interpretation of 'A slumber did my spirit seal' and have concluded that they were inspired by his love of Dorothy (Coleridge said of the poem, 'Most probably, in some gloomier moment he had fancied the moment in which his sister might die.') A difficulty here is that the Lucy of 'Three years she grew in sun and shower' is of 'stately height', which does not correspond to descriptions and portraits of Dorothy. Lucy may therefore have been a composite figure made up from several girls Wordsworth knew. The important point, however, is that knowledge of whether or not Lucy really existed is not necessary for an appreciation of the poems. Their power derives not from their possible association with actual persons but from their vivid representation of a particular kind of life, and their moving evocation of the poet's response to the ending of that life. The girl (or girls) portrayed in the poems seems isolated from the rest of humanity and has an unusually intimate relationship with nature. Death is seen as the inevitable conclusion of that relationship; the girl is finally absorbed by nature and becomes part of its eternal life. But there is a tension in the poems between acceptance of the girl's death and an unconcealed, poignantly evoked sense of loss. The poems are justly regarded as among Wordsworth's greatest achievements. Despite – it might be more accurate to say because of – their simplicity of language the poems are rich suggestive and have remarkable emotional depth and complexity.

In 'Strange fits of passion' the poet tells of a journey he once made to Lucy's cottage. During the journey he fixes his eye on the descending moon which, as he nears his destination, suddenly vanishes behind the cottage roof. The disappearance of the moon somehow gives rise to the fear that Lucy may be dead (this is the 'strange fit of passion' referred to in the opening line). This reaction appears irrational, but in recognizing Lucy's mortality the poet shows an awareness of reality that was previously absent. That before this moment of revelation he had been the victim of a delusion is first suggested in the second stanza:

> *When she I loved looked every day*
> *Fresh as a rose in June,*
> *I to her cottage bent my way,*
> *Beneath an evening moon.*

In the Lucy poems the girl's closeness to nature is suggested by recurrent natural imagery. Here the comparison with the rose serves also to evoke her beauty and, more significantly, the inevitability that this beauty will fade. The lover, however, did not think of this possibility; to him Lucy was everlasting and she looked like a rose in June 'every day'. His illusion prevented recognition of what happens to the rose once June is over. The use of the past tense is itself evidence of Lucy's mortality: '*When* she I loved looked every day' – the clear implication is that she looks like this no longer. The 'evening moon' similarly suggests changeability, a significance that is reinforced by the emphasis on its descent. Ironically the poet gazes fixedly at the sinking moon but (until the final stanza) remains ignorant of the transitoriness it symbolizes. As he eagerly approaches his lover's cottage ('With quickening pace my horse drew nigh/ Those paths so near to me') the description of the descending moon begins to carry the suggestion of a threat:

> *The sinking moon to Lucy's cot*
> *Came near, and nearer still.*

As in other Lucy poems, the girl lives surrounded by nature. The poet passes an orchard-plot and then ascends a hill to reach her cottage. As he nears his destination he is in a trance-like state similar to that described in the opening stanza of the final Lucy poem, 'A slumber did my spirit seal':

> *In one of those sweet dreams I slept,*
> *Kind Nature's gentlest boon!*
> *And all the while my eyes I kept*
> *On the descending moon.*
>
> *My horse moved on; hoof after hoof*
> *He raised, and never stopped . . .*

The repetition of 'hoof after hoof' and the assonance of 'hoof', 'moved' and 'moon' create a strange, hypnotic effect; Geoffrey Hartman calls it a feeling of 'motion approaching yet never quite attaining its end'. It is as if the lover is blissfully unaware of time and therefore of mortality, even though the sinking moon, on which his eyes continue to be fixed and which ironically helps to induce his reverie, is an insistent reminder of both. Appropriately, it is the sudden disappearance of the moon which breaks the trance and shocks the poet into consciousness of the inescapability of death:

> *'O mercy!' to myself I cried,*
> *'If Lucy should be dead!'*

The poet had watched the moon's descent but had not foreseen that this process must end with the moon dropping out of sight behind the horizon. When it does, its unexpected disappearance impresses upon him the inevitability of change and, by a convincing process of association, reminds him of Lucy's mortality. In the original manuscript version of the poem there is an additional stanza in which the episode becomes a foreshadowing of Lucy's actual death, reinforcing the validity of the poet's fear:

> *I told her this: her laughter light*
> *Is ringing in my ears:*
> *And when I think upon that night*
> *My eyes are dim with tears.*

In 'She dwelt among the untrodden ways' reference to Lucy's death becomes explicit. The poem begins by recalling her life, emphasizing her remoteness from human society and contrasting intimacy with nature:

> *She dwelt among the untrodden ways*
> *Beside the springs of Dove.*

A peculiar characteristic of these poems is that, although the intensity of the poet's love for her is unmistakable, Lucy herself remains an elusive figure. The reference to Lucy living beside the River Dove seems a precise enough detail, but Wordsworth apparently knew rivers of this name in Derbyshire, Yorkshire and Westmorland. The word 'Dove' may have been chosen because of its associations with gentleness and beauty (just as 'springs' suggests Lucy had a fresh, life-giving vitality), but the vagueness of location is also consistent with the other Lucy poems, which suggest that rather than belonging to a particular place Lucy was at one with the whole of nature.

The poet emphasizes next that Lucy's qualities were appreciated by very few and then in the second stanza uses vivid imagery to develop his point:

> *A violet by a mossy stone*
> *Half hidden from the eye!*
> *– Fair as a star, when only one*
> *Is shining in the sky.*

The image of the half-hidden violet suggests how Lucy was unnoticed by the world and reinforces her association with nature. Like the rose image in the previous poem, the comparison also evokes her beauty while at the same time implying its vulnerability (the 'mossy stone' has been seen by some readers as a gravestone, strengthening the suggestion of death). The image of a solitary shining star, while stressing again Lucy's remoteness, contrasts with the violet metaphor in its implication of outstanding, unrivalled splendour. The simile appears to embody the idea that while Lucy was unremarkable to others she was of supreme significance to the poet. The first two lines of the concluding stanza continue the emphasis on the world's indifference to Lucy, reflected in the unemotional, matter-of-fact description of her death ('When Lucy ceased to be'). But the poet's acute sense of loss is then movingly conveyed by the unexpected outburst of grief with which the poem ends. The language is simple and direct but charged with emotion:

> *But she is in her grave and oh,*
> *The difference to me!*

'Three years she grew' traces Lucy's growth under the direct healthful influence of nature. In the opening stanza the narrative voice quickly becomes that of 'Nature' herself:

> *Three years she grew in sun and shower*
> *Then Nature said, 'A lovelier flower*
> *On earth was never sown;*
> *This Child I to myself will take;*

> *She shall be mine, and I will make*
> *A Lady of my own.'*

As in the previous two poems Lucy is compared to a flower. The image has less suggestion of mortality than previously, but the idea of death is unquestionably present in the fourth line, with its reference to nature 'taking' Lucy. In fact the reader may well begin by believing the first four lines to mean that Lucy died when she was three years old. The conclusion of the stanza, however, suggests that such an interpretation would be incorrect; nature intends to make a 'Lady' of Lucy (and later in the poem there is a reference to the swelling of her 'virgin bosom' – l. 33). Lucy is therefore to be seen as a favoured individual who received the full benefits of nature's influence as she grew to maturity. The suggestion of death is significant, however, and is to recur in the poem, culminating in Lucy's actual death at the end. The impression is given that a close relationship with nature is a kind of death because it entails an existence which is close to the eternal sources of life and therefore free of the limitations of human mortality. Death itself is the ultimate consummation of this relationship.

Nature's intentions towards Lucy are elaborated upon in the second stanza:

> *'Myself will to my darling be*
> *Both law and impulse: and with me*
> *The Girl, in rock and plain,*
> *In earth and heaven, in glade and bower,*
> *Shall feel an overseeing power*
> *To kindle or restrain.'*

There is an antithetical pattern in the poem that begins with the reference to 'sun and shower' in the opening line and is most noticeable in this verse: 'law and impulse', 'rock and plain', 'earth and heaven', 'glade and bower', 'kindle or restrain'. The effect is to suggest that the complex process of natural, organic growth involves an interaction of opposing forces, an idea that is found elsewhere in Wordsworth's poetry (in 'The Prelude' he recalls, 'I grew up/ Fostered alike by beauty and by fear' – Book I, ll. 305–6). 'Rock and plain' and 'glade and bower' also enable us to picture the child growing up amidst natural surroundings and suggest exposure to the whole of nature. 'Earth and heaven', however, again carries a clear implication of death; the phrase seems to mean that the girl shall feel nature's presence in death as well as in life.

The third stanza is again built around a conjunction of opposites.

Lucy will have the vitality of a fawn racing across lawns and up mountains but she will also have another, contrasting gift:

> *And hers shall be the breathing balm,*
> *And hers the silence and the calm*
> *Of mute insensate things.*

Wordsworth valued both exuberant physical delight in the natural world and quiet communion with its inner peace, and saw them as essential elements in the human response to nature. In 'Tintern Abbey' he recalls the time when 'like a roe/ I bounded o'er the mountains' (ll. 67–8) but speaks also of 'that serene and blessed mood' when

> *we are laid asleep*
> *In body, and become a living soul:*
> *While with an eye made quiet by the power*
> *Of harmony, and the deep power of joy,*
> *We see into the life of things.*
>
> ll. 45–9

Lucy's serenity derives from a similar feeling of unity with the vital forces of the universe. But 'the silence and the calm/ Of mute insensate things' are also the tranquillity of death, and are the clearest suggestion so far that for nature's work to be complete, for Lucy to be fully at one with her, Lucy must die.

The next three stanzas continue to describe the way in which the forces of nature 'mould' Lucy (l. 23) in such a way as to bring her even closer to them. Again we have the sense of contrasting natural elements contributing to this development; Lucy is exposed to 'the motions of the Storm' (l. 22) as well as the murmuring of rivulets. Lucy is not a passive participant in this process but actively responds to the life she grows to perceive in nature: 'The stars of midnight shall be dear/ To her', and she will 'lean her ear' to the sound of streams (l. 26). As in other Lucy poems the picture created is of a girl experiencing nature in seclusion ('In many a secret place' – l. 27).

The final stanza, in which the narrator re-enters the poem, brings a dramatic change of perspective:

> *Thus Nature spake – The work was done –*
> *How soon my Lucy's race was run!*
> *She died, and left to me*
> *This heath, this calm, and quiet scene;*
> *The memory of what has been,*
> *And never more will be.*

Lucy's death is directly spoken of for the first time and there is an emphasis on the tragedy of that death. The bereaved poet reflects sadly on the brevity of her life and on the irretrievable loss he has suffered. The natural landscape, which in the earlier part of the poem had been linked with Lucy's vibrant energy, now evokes a sense of desolation because she is missing from it and 'never more will be'. At the same time, the strength of Lucy's association with a familiar landscape is something from which the poet can draw consolation; the heath, 'this calm and quiet scene', will endure and as well as being a painful reminder of his loss will be a lasting source of memories. Also running counter to the poet's grief is the notion that has been implicit throughout the poem: that Lucy's absorption by eternal nature was the inevitable, and fitting, end to her life. 'The work was done' and the reference to 'Lucy's race' now being 'run' imply a process that has reached its natural conclusion. Lucy is now truly at one with the non-human universe and shares the calm of the heath and of 'mute insensate things'. It is the achievement of the poem to give full recognition to the aptness of Lucy's death without minimizing in any way the poet's feeling of loss.

A similar duality of vision exists in 'A slumber did my spirit seal', the greatest of the Lucy poems. It is the shortest poem in the group and exemplifies Wordsworth's language at its most spare and simple. Nevertheless it is a poem of extraordinary ambiguity and suggestiveness and one that repays repeated scrutiny. John Beer describes it as 'a gnomic and reverberant statement, over which one might puzzle for ever, like a riddle of the Sphinx'. Most of the problems of interpretation hinge on the relationship between the poem's two stanzas:

> *A slumber did my spirit seal;*
> *I had no human fears:*
> *She seemed a thing that could not feel*
> *The touch of earthly years.*
>
> *No motion has she now, no force;*
> *She neither hears nor sees;*
> *Rolled round in earth's diurnal course,*
> *With rocks, and stones, and trees.*

In a stimulating analysis of this poem A. P. Rossiter drew attention to the possibility of two opposite and apparently irreconcilable interpretations. In one reading (and this is the interpretation broadly followed by most critics) the two stanzas contrast the poet's state of mind before and after his loved one's death. The first stanza tells of the deluded belief he once had that she was immortal. 'Slumber' implies a dream-like state from which he would eventually awake, recalling the poet's reverie as he approached Lucy's cottage in 'Strange fits of passion'. 'Seal' similarly suggests that he was enveloped in a false security from which reality was excluded, the recurrent sibilants of the line reinforcing the serenity. As he now recognizes, he was foolish to have no 'human fears' because the woman *was* a human being and therefore subject to mortality. He blindly thought of her not as human but as a 'thing' to which the normal conditions of earthly human existence did not apply ('seemed' expresses the illusory nature of this perception). The second stanza then registers the shock of her death, which has destroyed the poet's delusion and forced him to acknowledge reality. She is now utterly devoid of life, unable to hear, move or see. Buried in the earth, she is as dead as rocks or stones (ironically, she has now become the 'thing' he took her to be in the first stanza). The poet's cruel loss has given him a new awareness of the impersonal forces which govern the universe; the unfeeling inexorability of these forces is reflected in the use of the coldly scientific word 'diurnal'.

In the second interpretation the entire poem, not just the final stanza, describes the poet's reaction to the woman's death. The first stanza is in the past tense because it recollects a moment of visionary insight experienced after his loved one had died; the second stanza elaborates on what he sensed during this experience and is in the present tense because he believes that his vision revealed to him a still pertaining truth. Viewed in this light the tone of the poem becomes much more positive. Although the woman was dead the poet had a blissful sense of her essential immortality; he knew that she was free of human constraints and had become part of a larger transcendent reality. She was now 'a thing that could not feel/ The touch of earthly years'. In the second stanza the poet reflects that although the woman is now humanly inert ('No motion has she now, no force') she is at one with the vital generating forces of the universe ('*Rolled* round in earth's diurnal course'). Seen from this perspective the last two lines have a majestic sweep which suggests that her death was an ennobling experience.

These two readings of the poem are not incompatible but mutually illuminating. In fact it is possible to take something from each of the interpretations and produce a third reading, in which the poet's delusion about Lucy's immortality is destroyed by her death but the pain caused by the shattering of this delusion is offset by the recognition that the loved one has, by dying, attained another kind of immortality. The important point, however, is that none of these readings is more 'true' than the others; an intelligent response to the poem must accept its essential ambivalence. The ambiguity of the poem confirms what the other Lucy poems suggest: Wordsworth's acceptance of death was threatened by his acute sense of the grief and distress it causes to the bereaved.

'I travelled among unknown men', written two years after the rest of the poems in the group, lacks their compression and intensity but is consistent with them in its portrayal of Lucy as a child of nature. Lucy is not mentioned in the first two stanzas, which describe the poet's travels abroad and his determination to remain now in the England that he loves. His absence from the country has brought home the strength of his attachment to it ('Nor, England! did I know till then/ What love I bore to thee'). The poet's sense of alienation in foreign surroundings is evident in the reference to 'unknown men' and in the intentional vagueness of 'lands beyond the sea' (l. 2); he describes his experiences there as a 'melancholy dream' (l. 5). In the second half of the poem it becomes clear that his affection for England derives in great measure from the memories of Lucy it revives. When his love is recollected it is inevitably seen in the context of a natural landscape:

> *Among thy mountains did I feel*
> *The joy of my desire.*

Lucy is then recalled turning a spinning-wheel by the fireside. In all the poems this is the only occasion on which we learn of Lucy engaged in an indoor activity (although her cottage features in 'Strange fits of passion'), and if we view the poems as a coherent group the image perhaps strikes a slightly discordant note – though it does carry an appropriate suggestion of rural tranquillity.

More characteristic is the poem's conclusion:

> *Thy mornings showed, thy nights concealed,*
> *The bowers where Lucy played;*
> *And thine too is the last green field*
> *That Lucy's eyes surveyed.*

The second line of the stanza evokes a childhood surrounded and protected by nature. That Lucy's death is then alluded to rather than directly mentioned is in keeping with the serenity of the poem's conclusion. The sharp sense of loss evident in the other Lucy poems is absent; after the inner struggles of these earlier poems the poet appears to have reached a total acceptance of Lucy's quiet return to nature.

'Michael'

'Michael' is the finest of the rustic poems in the *Lyrical Ballads*.

Wordsworth describes it as a 'Pastoral Poem', which suggests an association with a tradition that originated in classical times. The conventional pastoral presented a nostalgic vision of the life of shepherds, portraying a peaceful, carefree existence in idyllic surroundings. During the eighteenth century, however, rural life was depicted with increasing realism, and in 1783 George Crabbe's 'The Village' was specifically intended to 'paint the cot/ As truth will paint it and as bards will not'. In 'Michael' the shepherd of the title is viewed with sympathy and admiration but without sentimentality. The vivid, detailed account of his working life and the financial misfortunes he suffers gives the poem an impressive authenticity. The poem is narrated with simplicity, as were the other rustic stories we have discussed, but the narrative voice is Wordsworth's own, and the conversational garrulity of some of the other poems is absent. The unforced naturalness of the language gives the poem a quiet power which is reinforced by the restrained, dignified movement of the blank verse.

The opening of the poem emphasizes the seclusion of its setting. But as so often in Wordsworth isolation from other human beings facilitates a closer communion with the natural world:

> *but they*
> *Who journey thither find themselves alone*
> *With a few sheep, with rocks and stones, and kites*
> *That overhead are sailing in the sky.*

ll. 9–12

The word 'alone' is immediately negated by what follows; the traveller to this spot finds himself surrounded by living proof of a vital, harmonious reality. Michael when he is introduced has a clear affinity with this reality. He and the elements of nature effortlessly coalesce:

> *he had been alone*
> *Amid the heart of many thousand mists,*
> *That came to him, and left him, on the heights.*

ll. 58–60

Michael's interaction with his natural surroundings helps to shape his moral character. Just as the Old Cumberland Beggar reminded villagers of their past charity and thereby promoted them to further acts of virtue, so the landscape acts as a record of Michael's past achievements and exercises a positive influence on his future behaviour. The fields and hills

> *had impressed*
> *So many incidents upon his mind*

Of hardship, skill or courage, joy or fear;
Which, like a book, preserved the memory
Of the dumb animals, whom he had saved,
Had fed or sheltered . . .

ll. 67–72

Michael's love of the natural world is augmented by an equally strong love for another human being when a son is born to him. Luke is the source of a new, intensely felt pleasure (he is Michael's 'heart and his heart's joy' – l. 152), but there are also ominous suggestions that this human affection is a threat to the tranquillity Michael has achieved through his peaceful accord with nature. Luke is born when Michael is apparently ready for death ('With one foot in the grave' – l. 90) and his arrival produces in his father disturbing 'stirrings of inquietude' (l. 149). The love Michael has for him is significantly described as 'Exceeding' (l. 151).

Nevertheless, Michael's dedication to his family is valued by Wordsworth, who explained in a letter to Charles James Fox that when he created the character he was thinking of the 'rapidly disappearing' class of 'small independent proprietors' who possessed strong 'domestic affections' allied to a profound attachment to the land that they worked. In another letter, to Thomas Poole, he gave the following explanation of his intentions:

I have attempted to give the picture of a man, of strong mind and lively sensibility, agitated by two of the most powerful affections of the human heart; the parental affection, and the love of property, landed property, including the feelings of inheritance, home and personal and family independence.

The lamp which hangs in the family's cottage and burns far into the night serves as an emblem for their collective providence and industry:

The light was famous in its neighbourhood,
And was a public symbol of the life
That thrifty pair had lived.

ll. 129–31

Michael's small but hard-earned piece of property, which he hopes to pass on to his son, is threatened when his nephew, for whom he has stood surety, falls into debt. Michael may have to sell some of his land. The news is a crushing blow; the lines describing the effect upon Michael have an appropriate flatness of tone and inert rhythm:

This unlooked-for claim,
At the first hearing, for a moment took

> *More hope out of his life than he supposed*
> *That any old man ever could have lost.*

ll. 217–20

In order to preserve Luke's inheritance and his family's proud independence Michael decides to settle the debt by sending his son to the city to work for a prosperous relative. Before Luke leaves he is taken by his father to lay the corner-stone for a new sheep-fold. Michael vows that when Luke returns he will find the sheep-fold completed. The sheep-fold, the central symbol of the poem, will therefore be (as Michael says) a 'covenant' between them (l. 414), representing the love between father and son, their hopes for the future and their mutual commitment to maintaining the family's farm and lands.

Luke, however, proves unworthy of his father's trust. He falls into dissolute ways and eventually brings such disgrace upon himself that he has to leave the country. Significantly, his decline takes place in the city, away from the beneficial influence of nature; as elsewhere in Wordsworth, urban society is associated with corruption. Luke's moral disintegration occupies a mere six lines of the poem (ll. 442–7), and Wordsworth's principal interest is clearly the effect it has upon Michael. Like many other Wordsworth characters, Michael shows tremendous courage and endurance in the face of adversity. He is sustained by his continued devotion to his 'small inheritance' (l. 459):

> *There is a comfort in the strength of love;*
> *'Twill make a thing endurable, which else*
> *Would overset the brain, or break the heart . . .*

ll. 448–50

His intimate contact with the natural landscape continues, and he 'still looked up to sun and cloud,/ And listened to the wind' (ll. 456–7). Moreover, the 'love' referred to above encompasses continued love of his son as well as love of property.

Michael's intermittent attempts to complete the sheep-fold signify that his hope that Luke will remember their covenant and fulfil his father's original expectations is never completely extinguished. However, Michael's visits to the sheep-fold often bear witness to his quiet despair:

> *and 'tis believed by all*
> *That many and many a day he thither went,*
> *And never lifted up a single stone.*

ll. 464–6

The sheep-fold thus takes on at the close of the poem a dual significance: originally a symbol of the love between Michael and his son, Michael's continued commitment to its completion indicates the enduring power of that love; but the work is never finished and the straggling heaps of stones left behind when Michael dies are a lasting reminder of the grief and disillusionment he suffered because of his son's betrayal. The contrasting suggestions of the sheep-fold image contribute to the ambivalence of the poem's final lines:

> *yet the oak is left*
> *That grew beside their door; and the remains*
> *Of the unfinished Sheep-fold may be seen*
> *Beside the boisterous brook of Green-head Ghyll.*

ll. 479–82

The sad conclusion to Michael's story – after he and his wife have died their lands are taken over by a stranger and their cottage is subsequently pulled down – is offset by a recognition of the abiding life that is in nature, represented by the hardy oak tree and the boisterous brook.

'Tintern Abbey'

'Lines Composed a Few Miles above Tintern Abbey on Revisiting the Banks of the Wye during a Tour' appeared at the end of the first edition of *Lyrical Ballads* and was written later than the other poems in the volume. The most intensely personal of the poems in the first *Lyrical Ballads* (the Lucy poems were in the second volume), 'Tintern Abbey' heralded a new preoccupation with the poet's inner life. It is the first major work to be explicitly autobiographical and thus begins a sequence of great poems that culminates in 'The Prelude'. It expresses some of Wordsworth's central ideas about nature, perception and spiritual growth.

In the poem's opening verse paragraph (ll. 1–22) Wordsworth may appear at first to be uncharacteristically adopting the approach of a traditional poet of nature, offering us a pictorial description of a rural scene in the conventional eighteenth-century manner. Closer analysis however reveals the extent to which the landscape described to us is in fact a projection of the poet's own mood. To begin with, there is a repeated emphasis on his presence: 'again I hear', 'Once again/ Do I behold', 'Once again I see'. These quotations by themselves might suggest that Wordsworth is merely a passive receiver of sensory impressions, but the paragraph as a whole shows that he has carefully organized the details of what he sees and hears in such a way as to stress the tranquil harmony of the scene. This is significant because it means that the landscape becomes an emblem for the unity that Wordsworth perceives in nature and also because it prepares us for the account in the second verse paragraph of what Wordsworth's mental image of the landscape (carried in the memory) has meant to him in the years since his last visit. The various elements of the scene blend effortlessly with one another: the lofty cliffs 'connect/ The landscape with the quiet of the sky' (a connection that is strengthened by the effective use of enjambment); the plots of cottage-ground are not rigidly separated but are 'clad in one green hue' and merge with the surrounding woodland ('lose themselves/ 'Mid groves and copses'); the hedgerows similarly seem to be 'hardly hedge-rows' but 'little lines/ of sportive wood run wild'. The hedgerows and the cottage plots are evidence of quiet, unobtrusive human activity, and the coalescence of the human and inanimate elements of the landscape is further suggested by the farms which are 'Green to the very door' and the wreaths of smoke which rise gently above the trees. The tranquillity of the scene receives repeated emphasis; in addition to the 'quiet of the sky' and the smoke drifting upwards 'in silence' Wordsworth refers to the 'soft inland murmur' of the River Wye. The opening verse paragraph thus evokes a meditative calm suited to the next stage of the poem, in which Wordsworth turns away from the external scene and concentrates upon an explicit exploration of his own consciousness.

In this second section (ll. 22–49) Wordsworth considers what he has gained from the memory of his first visit to the Wye valley five years previously. His recollections of the landscape have had a therapeutic effect, bringing him 'tranquil restoration' in 'hours of weariness'. Significantly, this world-weariness is specifically associated with urban life: ''mid the din/ Of towns and cities'. Anxiety and despondency are experienced when the poet is away from the soothing influence of nature ('din' is in clear contrast to the quietness of the previous verse paragraph). He also attributes to his remembrances of the Wye valley a positive, albeit unconscious, influence upon his moral growth (ll. 30–35), an influence which has encouraged 'acts/ Of kindness and of love'. Wordsworth often suggests that exposure to, and reflection upon, the 'beauteous forms' of nature is morally beneficial – the doctrine seen at its most explicit in 'The Tables Turned':

> *One impulse from a vernal wood*
> *May teach you more of man,*
> *Of moral evil and of good,*
> *Than all the sages can.*

ll. 21–4

The third and most profound gift is a 'serene and blessed mood' which enables him to 'see into the life of things' (ll. 35–49). Wordsworth is describing here a state of heightened perception in which he is aware not of the material forms of nature but of an inner life force which permeates the natural world and exists within himself also. This experience does not involve the senses; in particular, the eye is specifically said to be 'made quiet by the power/ Of harmony'. Communing with a larger reality means that he is no longer aware of his bodily self:

> *Until, the breath of this corporeal frame*
> *And even the motion of our human blood*
> *Almost suspended, we are laid asleep*
> *In body, and become a living soul . . .*

At such moments the world ceases to be oppressive and problematic; the poet is released from the doubts and worries that sometimes afflict him and experiences a comprehensive understanding of the nature of things: 'the heavy and the weary weight/ Of all this unintelligible world,/ Is lightened'. The account of this 'blessed mood' recalls other descriptions of visionary experience in Wordsworth's poetry. The experiences usually involve a state of suspension (in 'There was a boy', for example, the moment of insight occurred as the boy 'hung/ Listening'); they occur during periods of silence or tranquillity (evoked here by words such as 'serene', 'asleep' and 'quiet'), and they produce a blissful sense of the ultimate unity of the universe, and of being part of that unity.

The three benefits Wordsworth believes he has gained from his re-collections of the Wye valley illustrate the importance he attached to memory. Through the exercise of memory pleasurable experiences of the past were still available to him. Moreover, these experiences often have their most profound effect *after* they have been absorbed and contemplated. Thus remembering the harmonious forms of the Wye valley induces a mood in which the essential harmony of all things can be perceived. (Another example is 'I wandered lonely as a cloud', where the daffodils are valued less for the immediate pleasure they brought than for the later occasions when they 'flash upon that inward eye'.)

Wordsworth has made bold assertions about the influence the scenery of the Wye valley has had upon him, but this second verse paragraph also contains suggestions of an underlying doubt. His response to the landscape has 'perhaps' encouraged acts of kindness and love (l. 31), and the beautiful countryside 'may' be responsible for moments when the world is perceived with exceptional clarity (l. 36). The uncertainty becomes stronger in the next verse paragraph (ll. 49–57): 'If this/ Be but a vain belief'. Wordsworth may mean by this that he is not sure if his visionary experiences derive from his recollections of the Wye valley; but another, more serious doubt seems also to be present: whether he is right in thinking that during these experiences he really does 'see into the life of things'. He clearly has a desperate need to believe that there are occasions when he is able to grasp the meaning of a world which at other times is 'unintelligible', but he is honest enough to admit the difficulty of interpreting with confidence experiences of such transience and intangibility. He then understandably returns to what he *can* be sure of – the solace to be gained from memories of the Wye valley when wearied by 'the fretful stir/ Unprofitable, and the fever of the world'. Wordsworth reiterates here the point that was made at the beginning of the previous verse paragraph (ll. 22–30). The poem as a whole contains several such repetitions, as well as moving back and forth between past and present; we feel we are following closely the course of Wordsworth's thoughts as he attempts to clarify and evaluate what nature has meant to him.

The present is returned to at the beginning of the next verse paragraph (ll. 58–111): 'And now . . .' The poet's uncertainty is again evident in the reference to his 'sad perplexity'. He seeks reassurance from 'pleasing thoughts/ That in this moment there is life and food/ For future years'. Again he is asserting that past experiences are a source of regeneration, but there is still an element of doubt: 'And so I dare to hope . . .' This brief glimpse into the future is followed by an imaginative recreation of his past life that reaches as far back as the 'boyish days' of his childhood. He traces the evolution of his relationship with nature and considers the gains and losses. He has experienced unthinking, physical enjoyment ('glad animal movements'), intense emotional and sensory pleasure ('aching joys . . . dizzy raptures') and finally conscious realization of the invisible force that unifies and impels the whole of nature (the 'motion' and 'spirit' that 'rolls through all things'). The poem has again turned back on itself; the final phase in his development mentioned by Wordsworth is essentially the same as the 'blessed mood' referred to earlier when he felt able to 'see into the life of things'. There is more confidence now about the nature of what is perceived during these moments of vision but there is also in this verse paragraph a suggestion of a different kind of doubt. In comparing his past and present selves Wordsworth hopes that the development from the emotional intensity of his youth to the more reflective response to nature of adulthood has been a positive one. That he has some uncertainty over this however is indicated by 'I would believe', which gives the impression of Wordsworth *forcing* himself to believe. (For a fuller discussion of this passage see the section on 'Nature' in Chapter 7.)

The final verse paragraph (ll. 111–59) surprises us by revealing the presence alongside Wordsworth of his sister Dorothy. However, it soon becomes apparent that her principal role in the poem is as a reincarnation of Wordsworth's former self. Her 'wild eyes' and 'wild ecstasies' are a reminder of the 'aching joys' and 'dizzy raptures' of his youth. Again the recollection of his passionate enthusiasm for nature is accompanied by a sense of loss:

> *Oh! yet a little while*
> *May I behold in thee what I was once . . .*

He believes that nature will be to Dorothy the restorative force that it has been to him, enabling her to withstand the harsher aspects of human society and the 'dreary intercourse of daily life'. He expects her relationship with nature to change as his has done, maturing into a 'sober pleasure'. This new preoccupation with the future continues with Wordsworth's anticipation of his own death (ll. 147 ff.). He hopes that he will live on in Dorothy's memories of the Wye valley. At its close the poem returns to the external scene, the references to the 'green pastoral landscape', 'steep woods' and 'lofty cliffs' echoing the opening description. But just as the quiet heath at the end of 'Three years she grew' was to Wordsworth evocative of Lucy's former presence, so this landscape is now to the reader inseparable from Wordsworth's varied and complex response to it.

4. Poems 1800–1807

For most of the period covered in this chapter Wordsworth was still at the peak of his creative powers. Critics often speak of the 'great decade' from 1797 to 1807, though the decline in the quality of his verse arguably begins as early as 1806. Most of the poems written in the years 1800–7 were published in *Poems in Two Volumes* (1807). Many of Wordsworth's best-known shorter poems date from this period, including 'The Solitary Reaper', 'I wandered lonely as a cloud' and 'To the Cuckoo'. He also wrote a smaller number of longer pieces, notably 'Resolution and Independence' and the Immortality Ode. Many of the poems were auto-biographical, but he also found inspiration in the experiences of others (as in 'The Solitary Reaper') and made use of his sister Dorothy's Journals ('I wandered lonely as a cloud' is a particularly interesting example of this). Greatly influenced by his reading of Milton, he wrote for the first time a number of sonnets, including 'Composed upon Westminster Bridge'. This chapter adopts a similar approach to the previous two and analyses a selection of major poems from the period.

'Resolution and Independence' and 'The Solitary Reaper'

We know from Dorothy Wordsworth's Journal that 'Resolution and Independence' is based upon an incident which took place on 3 October 1800. William and Dorothy met an 'old man almost double', who told them that he had formerly been a leech-gatherer but owing to the increasing scarcity of leeches had abandoned this occupation and was now a beggar. Wordsworth's version of the episode contains two significant alterations. Firstly, he omits Dorothy. The encounter with the old man becomes an intensely personal experience; as is usually the case with Wordsworth's solitaries, the leech-gatherer's importance derives from the impact he makes on the poet's consciousness. The second change is that in Wordsworth's poem the man perseveres as a leech-gatherer despite his difficulties. This is an essential alteration because he is seen by the poet as an example of stoical endurance in the face of suffering and adversity.

The opening stanzas describe an exhilarating natural scene on the morning after a storm. The landscape is teeming with energetic life. The impression of exuberant activity is reinforced by the use of the present tense in the first two verses and also by personification: 'The sky rejoices' in 'the morning's birth' (l. 9). There is the characteristic Wordsworthian emphasis on natural unity, with the various elements in the scene responding to each other's presence. The jay answers the magpie's chatter, and as the hare runs on the wet earth the little mist it creates seems to follow it about. The poet, who enters the poem in the third stanza, at first feels part of this rapturous harmony. The ambiguity of 'I saw the hare that raced about with joy' (the joy could be the hare's or the poet's) is appropriate, suggesting the correspondence of mood between Wordsworth and his natural surroundings. As in 'Tintern Abbey' we see the restorative power of nature banishing the vexations associated with human society:

> *My old remembrances went from me wholly;*
> *And all the ways of men, so vain and melancholy.*

ll. 20–21

Forgetting 'the ways of men' also means temporary freedom from the restrictions of adulthood. His immediate, spontaneous delight in nature is like that of a child; he describes himself as feeling 'as happy as a boy' (l. 18).

In the fourth stanza, however, there is a sudden reversal of mood and Wordsworth is plunged into depression. The extreme change in the natural world referred to at the beginning of the poem, when a violent overnight storm was followed by a 'calm and bright' morning, is now seen as prefiguring the poet's experience. In Wordsworth's case the pattern is reversed, and contentment is succeeded by the onset of mental turbulence (though there is a restoration of tranquillity at the end of the poem). He believes the instability he describes is something all human beings are subject to, as his use of the second person plural indicates:

> *As high as we have mounted in delight*
> *In our dejection do we sink as low.*

ll. 24–5

He experiences an onslaught of doubts and anxieties, and the rhythm at the close of the stanza is appropriately disturbed:

> *Dim sadness – and blind thoughts, I knew not,*
> *nor could name.*

l. 28

The 'fears and fancies' that oppress him become more specific in the next stanza. Earlier in the poem he had been able to forget the problems of human existence, the cares associated with the 'ways of men'. He had been an unthinking 'Child of earth', immersed in the pleasures of the present and oblivious of the passage of time. Now, however, the adult vision of life with its fearful concern for the future returns:

> *But there may come another day to me –*
> *Solitude, pain of heart, distress and poverty.*

ll. 34–5

The 'old remembrances' that had been temporarily put aside also re-appear. As he contemplates the transience of human happiness Wordsworth recalls the fate of other poets (stanza vii). Chatterton, appar-ently driven to despair by poverty, committed suicide, and much of the later life of Robert Burns ('Him who walked in glory and in joy') was characterized by anxiety and dissipation. He reflects that 'By our own spirits are we deified', meaning that the poet's pride and ecstasy are self-created. His 'spirits' are just as capable of driving him to the other extreme, to 'despondency and madness'.

Wordsworth's meeting with the leech-gatherer enables him to overcome his melancholy. The example given to him by the old man's attitude to life has such relevance to his own predicament that the en-counter might have been the result of divine intervention ('Now, whether it were by peculiar grace,/ A leading from above, a something given' – ll. 50–51). When the man is first seen he is significantly close to elemental forms of nature: 'Beside a pool bare to the eye of heaven' (l. 54). The celebrated images of the rock and the sea-beast in stanza ix reinforce the old man's oneness with the natural world as well as having several other appropriate implications. The comparison with a 'huge stone' suggests the leech-gatherer's strength, powers of endurance and great age; like the Old Cumberland Beggar he seems to exist outside the normal human time scale, appearing to be 'The oldest man ... that ever wore grey hairs' (l. 56). The simile also evokes a stability that is in marked contrast to the wild fluctuations of mood experienced by the poet. The sea-beast with which the rock (and therefore, indirectly, the leech-gatherer) is then compared reinforces the impression of elemental strength. The way in which the imagined sea-beast 'reposeth' on a shelf of rock or sand in order to sun itself underlines the old man's imperturbability. The two images also combine to suggest that the man occupies a kind of hinter-land between human and inanimate nature. His eerie calmness and immo-bility give rise to the image of a rock, but at the same time he is sufficiently 'endued with sense' to invite comparison with something living.

Wordsworth develops this idea in the next stanza (x), where he de-scribes the man as 'not all alive or dead'. His intentions are further clarified by a passage in the Preface to the 1815 edition of the collected poems:

The stone is endowed with something of the power of life to approximate it to the sea-beast; and the sea-beast stripped of some of its vital qualities to assimilate it to the stone: which intermediate image is thus treated for the purpose of bringing the original image, that of the stone, to a nearer resemblance to the figure and condition of the old Man; who is divested of so much of the indications of life and motion as to bring him to the point where the two objects unite and coalesce in just comparison.

The old man's appearance ('His body was bent double') suggests to Wordsworth that he has had to endure great suffering:

> *As if some dire constraint of pain, or rage*
> *Of sickness felt by him in times long past,*
> *A more than human weight upon his frame had cast.*

ll. 68–70

It is the leech-gatherer's strength in the face of exceptional ('more than human') adversity that is to have the greatest influence upon Wordsworth. The old man's imperviousness to suffering is suggested by another natural image, that of a cloud which seems oblivious to the winds that blow around it and steadfastly retains its identity ('And moveth all together, if it move at all' – l. 77).

The poet now engages the leech-gatherer in conversation (stanzas xii and xiii). Wordsworth's mundane questions and observations ('"This morning gives us promise of a glorious day" . . . "What occupation do you there pursue?"') enhance the credibility of the episode but also suggest that at this stage in their encounter he had not grasped the old man's significance. The leech-gatherer's mode of speech reflects his dignity, calmness and moral strength; it is 'measured' and 'stately',

> *Such as grave Livers do in Scotland use,*
> *Religious men, who give to God and man their dues.*

ll. 97–8

Again it is emphasized that he exists apart from – indeed is, superior to – common humanity: his 'lofty utterance' was 'above the reach/ Of ordinary men'. The content of the old man's speech is revealed in stanza xv. We learn that he exists by gathering leeches, and that this employment is 'hazardous and wearisome'. He has had 'many hardships' to endure and must rely on 'God's good help' and 'chance'. Thus although the leech-gatherer is a figure of rock-like strength Wordsworth does not minimize the deprivations and difficulties his way of life involves.

In stanza xvi we can sense Wordsworth moving towards an understanding of the old man's significance. His meeting with the leech-gatherer begins to take on the nature of a visionary experience; the old man's voice becomes like 'a stream/ Scarce heard' and the man himself like someone 'met within a dream'. The poet starts to perceive that the leech-gatherer can give him 'human strength'. But Wordsworth's deepening response to the old man is interrupted by the return of his 'former thoughts' (stanza xviii). Burdened again by anxiety and fear but realizing that through the leech-gatherer he may discover a means of combating his distress, he resumes speaking to the old man; there is a new urgency and profundity about his questioning: '"How is it that you live, and what is it you do?"' He is seeking not information about the man's occupation (which he has already been given) but an explanation of his attitude to life, the secret of his remarkable fortitude. The leech-gatherer's reply, however, expressed in verse that is deliberately flat and prosaic, is little more than a repetition of the harsh facts of his existence (stanza xviii). He tells the poet that the supply of leeches is steadily dwindling, '"Yet still I persevere, and find them where I may."' The insight into the old man's way of life that Wordsworth seeks comes not from what the man himself says but from the exercise of his own imagination. As the leech-gatherer speaks Wordsworth pursues 'thoughts within myself' (stanza xix). His vision of what the old man's life amounts to takes on clear and definite shape:

> *In my mind's eye I seemed to see him pace*
> *About the weary moors continually,*
> *Wandering about alone and silently.*

ll. 129–31

Wordsworth says that his thoughts about the leech-gatherer 'troubled' him. Contemplating the solitude and unremitting hardship the old man has to suffer evidently distresses him. At the same time, however, the man's imagined solitary wanderings signify his uncomplaining acceptance of his lot; he paces the moors both 'continually' and 'silently'. Moreover, he speaks to Wordsworth 'Cheerfully' (l. 135) and 'with a smile' (l. 120). Such strength of spirit and firmness of mind are stressed at the conclusion of the poem. Wordsworth believes the memory of the leech-gatherer will sustain him in future times of depression and doubt. The encounter has given him the 'human strength' he spoke of earlier, and the old man has become for him a lasting symbol of human endurance.

'The Solitary Reaper' describes the poet's reaction to another figure alone in a natural landscape. The idea for the poem came not from an experience of Wordsworth's but from a sentence in an account of a visit to Scotland written by a friend, Thomas Wilkinson: 'Passed a female who was reaping alone: she sung in Erse as she bended over her sickle; the sweetest human voice I ever heard: her strains were tenderly melancholy, and felt delicious, long after they were heard no more.' As Wordsworth acknowledged in a note, the last line of his poem borrows directly from Wilkinson's description. In Wordsworth's treatment of the incident the reaper's song becomes expressive of a profound harmony between man and nature.

The opening stanza of the poem repeatedly emphasizes the reaper's isolation: 'single', 'solitary', 'by herself', 'Alone'. But though she lacks human company her song, which fills the entire landscape, creates a bond with her natural surroundings:

> *O listen! for the Vale profound*
> *Is overflowing with the sound.*

'Overflowing' here is the first suggestion that the song transcends space and time and is seen by the poet as the manifestation of an eternal, all-pervading life force. This suggestion is taken up in the second stanza, where the geographical perspective of the poem is broadened still further; the girl's song is compared to a nightingale's 'Among Arabian sands' (this image also gives the song a mysterious, magical quality) and to a cuckoo's 'Breaking the silence of the seas/ Among the farthest Hebrides'. In the third stanza the song reaches back across the centuries; the poet wonders whether its subject is 'Familiar matter of today' or 'old, unhappy, far-off things,/ And battles long ago'. The concluding lines of the stanza link past and future, surmising that the reaper's song relates to the everlasting truths of human experience:

> *Some natural sorrow, loss, or pain,*
> *That has been, and may be again?*

Wordsworth realizes that the precise content of the song matters not ('Whate'er the theme . . .'). What is important is his response to it, his intuitive sense that the song expresses a fundamental unity between human beings and a still larger unity between man and the natural world. The deep impression that song makes upon him is evident in the way in which he listens to it 'motionless and still' – another reminder of how frequently in Wordsworth's poetry the most penetrating perceptions occur during moments of suspension. It is as if the poet is in touch with the infinite. As the reaper sang it seemed that 'her song could have no ending', and when he left the valley her song remained with him:

> *The music in my heart I bore,*
> *Long after it was heard no more.*

Just as the memory of the leech-gatherer was a perpetual source of strength, so the reaper's song will be an enduring reminder of ultimate harmony.

'I wandered lonely as a cloud' and 'To the Cuckoo'

As with 'Resolution and Independence', the incident upon which 'I wandered lonely as a cloud' is based is described in Dorothy Wordsworth's Journal. A comparison of Wordsworth's poem and Dorothy's Journal entry helps to clarify Wordsworth's intentions in writing his poem and reveals much about his poetic method. This is Dorothy's account of the experience:

(15 April 1802) . . . We saw a few daffodils close to the water-side. We fancied that the lake had floated the seeds ashore, and that the little colony had so sprung up. But as we went along there were more and yet more; and at last, under the boughs of the trees, we saw that there was a long belt of them along the shore, about the breadth of a country turnpike road. I never saw daffodils so beautiful. They grew among the mossy stones about and about them; some rested their heads upon these stones as on a pillow for weariness; and the rest tossed and reeled and danced, and seemed as if they verily laughed with the wind that blew upon them over the lake; they looked so gay, ever glancing, ever changing. This wind blew directly over the lake to them. There was here and there a little knot, and a few stragglers a few yards higher up; but they were so few as not to disturb the simplicity, and unity, and life of that one busy highway.

The most obvious alteration made by Wordsworth is that (as in his version of the encounter with the leech-gatherer) Dorothy is eliminated from the experience. In Wordsworth's poetry communion with the natural world is more deeply satisfying when enjoyed in solitude; indeed in several poems ('Tintern Abbey' and 'Resolution and Independence', for example) the poet seems to be in retreat from human society. Moreover, in Wordsworth the profoundest fulfilment often derives from solitary contemplation of an experience of nature *after* it has occurred. Dorothy records her immediate response to the daffodils, but in Wordsworth's poem the emphasis is upon the pleasure that comes from recollection of the incident. This helps to explain why in Dorothy's account the daffodils are more precisely observed; Wordsworth clearly made use of his sister's description (his poem is thought to have been written two years later), but there is no attempt to reproduce its exact detail ('some rested their heads upon these stones as on a pillow for weariness. . . . There was here and there a little knot, and a few stragglers a few yards higher up'). Wordsworth is much more interested in his own reaction to the daffodils, and in the *inner* reality of the flowers as opposed to their external appearance. They are seen in the poem as a reassuring manifestation of the fundamental order of nature, a significance only slightly hinted at in Dorothy's reference to the 'unity' of the scene.

Wordsworth expresses his isolation in the opening line of the poem but, as his decision to omit Dorothy from the incident indicates, it is not the absence of others that troubles him. He is rather 'lonely' in the sense that he feels separate from the world about him, a separateness that is emphasized by the comparison with a cloud 'That floats on high o'er vales and hills'. The daffodils, however, banish the poet's feeling of alienation by inducing a sudden responsiveness to the natural landscape. The flowers are first seen as a 'crowd' and then as a 'host', reflecting Wordsworth's growing awareness of the beautiful harmony of the scene. There is a similar heightening in 'Fluttering and dancing', the latter word (which recurs in the poem) emphasizing again the poet's recognition of the flowers' joyous unity. The comparison in the second stanza with 'the stars that shine/ And twinkle on the milky way' reinforces the delightful radiance of the golden daffodils and suggests their abundance. More significantly, the image produces an enormous broadening of perspective, associating the unity of the daffodils with the infinitely larger unity of the universe as a whole; a similar effect – though not intended to suggest so great an expansion – was achieved by the references to 'Arabian sands' and 'the farthest Hebrides' in 'The Solitary Reaper'.

In the third stanza the harmonious movement of the daffodils is shared by the waves of the lake, which 'danced' beside them; the waves also share the flowers' brightness (they are described as 'sparkling'). Wordsworth himself feels part of this joyful harmony and is no longer the lonely figure described at the beginning of the poem (he now has 'jocund company'). His aimlessness has also disappeared and his attention is now wholly engaged: 'I gazed and gazed'. What Wordsworth did not fully realize at the same time was that the immediate visual enjoyment afforded by the sight of the daffodils would be followed by a deeper, contemplative pleasure. The daffodils remain accessible to him through the exercise of memory and are therefore comparable to a store of treasure which the poet is able to draw upon (the imagery of wealth in this stanza gives an added significance to the earlier word 'golden'). The later experience is dependent upon imaginative power rather than sensory perception; the daffodils are seen with an 'inward eye'. Note that this 'inward eye' is said to be 'the bliss of solitude'; seeing 'into the life of things' (the quotation is from 'Tintern Abbey') is, for the adult at least, the result of quiet, solitary meditation. During these moments of visionary insight the poet is alone but (in contrast to his mood at the beginning of the poem) not 'lonely'. Blissfully aware of the essential harmony of nature, and of his own place in that harmony, he is able to join with the daffodils in their joyful dance:

> *And then my heart with pleasure fills,*
> *And dances with the daffodils.*

The daffodils are important, then, because they facilitate the perception of a larger reality. The cuckoo's song in 'To the Cuckoo' has a similar significance. To Wordsworth the song is an expression of the life force that permeates the whole of nature. It is a particularly apt symbol for this pervasive energy because, like the song of the solitary reaper, it fills the landscape:

> *From hill to hill it seems to pass,*
> *At once far off, and near.*

The reality which Wordsworth responds to in the cuckoo's song is a reality that transcends physical existence, something greater than the bird itself, and it is this that gives rise to the poet's question in the opening stanza:

> *O Cuckoo! shall I call thee Bird,*
> *Or but a wandering Voice?*

The cuckoo achieves through its song a ubiquitous presence; as Wordsworth explained in the 1815 Preface, his question 'dispossesses the creature almost of a corporeal existence'. The bird's full significance to the poet becomes clearer in the third stanza:

> *Though babbling only to the Vale,*
> *Of sunshine and of flowers,*
> *Thou bringest unto me a tale*
> *Of visionary hours.*

Again we note that it is the interaction between man and nature that is important to Wordsworth; without the poet's presence the cuckoo's song is simply 'babbling'.

Hearing the song prompts Wordsworth to recollect visionary experiences of the past, and the later stanzas of the poem reveal that these experiences took place during childhood. When he was a boy he responded directly to the inner life of nature, to the 'invisible' force of which the cuckoo's song is but one manifestation. As he listens to the bird now, he believes he experiences again his childhood response to it:

> *Even yet thou art to me*
> *No bird, but an invisible thing,*
> *A voice, a mystery . . .*

However, the words 'Even yet' indicate Wordsworth's recognition that his vision of the world *has* changed: that if he is able briefly to recapture his childhood vision it is *despite* the fact that now he is an adult he is also aware of the cuckoo as a mere material object, as a 'bird' rather than a 'mystery'. There is thus a mixture of defiance and longing in these lines; a longing to recover the child's perception of the world is coupled with a defiant assertion that this perception has not been completely lost to him.

In the fifth and sixth stanzas Wordsworth elaborates on the childhood experience:

> *that Cry*
> *Which made me look a thousand ways*
> *In bush, and tree and sky.*

> *To seek thee did I often rove*
> *Through woods and on the green;*
> *And thou wert still a hope, a love;*
> *Still longed for, never seen.*

The cuckoo's song helped stimulate the eager exploration of nature evoked so vividly in the early books of 'The Prelude'. Wordsworth's love of the song was a love of the life that is *in* nature, of something that was therefore 'never seen'. The repeated 'still' has an effect similar to that of 'Even yet' earlier; it implies that the poet's perception of things has altered since childhood, and that he is aware of this. The next stanza provides confirmation of this. Wordsworth speaks here of listening to the bird 'till I do beget/ That golden time again'. The visionary experiences of childhood were spontaneous and immediate, but such experiences are now dependent upon the exercise of memory. The ability to recover and re-experience the child's vision of nature gives Wordsworth intense pleasure, but there is inevitably an element of 'second best' about the adult experience. Moreover, the conventional adult conception of the world can never be wholly displaced, as the closing stanza makes clear:

> *O blessed Bird! the earth we pace*
> *Again appears to be*
> *An unsubstantial, faery place;*
> *This is fit home for Thee!*

Wordsworth reiterates here that the cuckoo's song stimulates an awareness of the inner reality of the material world, a reality which is much more important, and much more 'real', than that world's external appearance. However, this awareness is inhibited by the adult's enslavement to physical reality. Unable to experience a direct, unalloyed sense of nature's secret life, the earth can for the adult only *'appear'* to be 'An unsubstantial, faery place'.

'Composed upon Westminster Bridge, September 3, 1802'

Dislike of urban life is a recurring theme in Wordsworth's poetry. In 'Tintern Abbey' the act of remembering the tranquil beauty of the Wye valley brings welcome relief from 'the din/ Of towns and cities', and in 'Michael' the shepherd's son is corrupted by 'the dissolute city'. It may therefore appear surprising that Wordsworth should have written a sonnet in praise of London. In fact, however, a close study of the poem reveals that his approval of the city landscape is far from unqualified. Admiration of the city as seen at this particular moment is subtly balanced by an implied aversion to its usual character.

The former element in the poem is of course the one that receives the most explicit expression. The opening line immediately evokes a scene of breathtaking beauty: 'Earth has not anything to show more fair'. The city has an undoubted magnificence, and words such as 'majesty', 'splendour' and 'mighty' are used in association with it. The man-made constructions of the town blend appealingly with the natural beauty of the surrounding countryside:

> *Ships, towers, domes, theatres, and temples lie*
> *Open unto the fields, and to the sky ...*

In tracing the vein of counter-suggestion in the poem we might firstly note that London is viewed from a distance. The poet does not present himself as a participant in the life of a busy, populous town (one of many illuminating contrasts with William Blake's poem 'London' is that Blake views the city from its noisy, crowded streets). Seen from this vantage-point and at this time of the day (the early morning), London has an uncharacteristic tranquillity. It is the serenity of the scene that Wordsworth responds most strongly to, particularly at the close of the poem:

Ne'er saw I, never felt, a calm so deep!
The river glideth at his own sweet will:
Dear God! the very houses seem asleep;
And all that mighty heart is lying still!

ll. 11–14

The transience of this calm is suggested in the last two lines quoted. If the houses are asleep they must soon awake, and if the city is not dead the 'mighty heart' must resume beating. The city's physical beauty has a similar impermanence. The 'smokeless' air would not be noticed if the city's atmosphere were not usually polluted (Blake's poem, written about ten years earlier, refers to 'black'ning' churches). London is said to 'wear' the beauty of the morning like a 'garment', an image which implies that this beauty is both transitory and deceptive. Wordsworth is captivated by the loveliness of the morning scene but also thinks of it as a glittering veneer concealing a much less pleasant reality beneath.

'Ode: Intimations of Immortality from Recollections of Early Childhood'

The first four stanzas of the Immortality Ode were composed in 1802 and the remainder in 1804. The earlier part of the poem mourns the loss of the visionary power of childhood, while the later stanzas advance a theory of human growth in order to explain that loss and attempt to resolve the spiritual crisis faced by the poet by asserting the consolations of maturity. The poem is central to an understanding of the development of Wordsworth's life and art. In addition to being one of his most memorable affirmations of the significance of childhood experience, it helps to explain the decline in visionary intensity that characterizes his later poetry and, in its emphasis on the importance and the value of the 'philosophic mind', prepares us for the controlled detachment of these later works.

The poem's opening stanza looks back to a time when the natural world was transfigured by a 'celestial light'. Every natural object seemed more than itself because the poet was intuitively aware of, and responsive to, a life in and beyond nature. This childhood perception has been lost, and the desolation Wordsworth now feels is apparent in the bleak, monosyllabic directness of the stanza's closing line: 'The things which I have seen I now can see no more.' In stanza ii we see that the poet has an aesthetic appreciation of natural beauty (he knows that 'lovely is the Rose' and that 'Waters on a starry night/ Are beautiful and fair') but that this dispassionate admiration is inferior to what he knew before. The decline in his responsiveness to natural phenomena is evident in the flat, unemotional opening line: 'The Rainbow comes and goes'. The lines in which Wordsworth confronts his loss are again painfully direct:

> *But yet I know, where'er I go,*
> *That there hath past away a glory from the earth.*

The third stanza emphasizes that the harmony with the natural world Wordsworth felt as a child has been broken. The whole of nature seems united by the joy of springtime ('And with the heart of May/ Doth every Beast keep holiday'), but it is a unity from which he is excluded: 'To me alone there came a thought of grief'. He is determined to share again in the bliss of nature and defiantly asserts: 'I again am strong . . . No more shall grief of mine the season wrong.' There seems an element of desperation, however, in the plea to the 'Shepherd-boy' to fill his ears with shouts of joy. The poet hopes that exposure to the child's natural, unforced happiness will induce a similar elation. That in reality he is still alienated from the life around him is suggested by the opening of stanza iv. The 'blessed Creatures' call to 'each other' but, by implication, not to him. He continues to claim 'My heart is at your festival', but this is belied by the hesitation of 'I feel – I feel it all'. We do not find it surprising when melancholy overwhelms him again at the close of the stanza (ll. 51–7). The 'Tree', the 'field' and the 'pansy' now lack the transcendent reality, the 'celestial light', they possessed during his childhood and are reminders of his loss, speaking of 'something that is gone'.

In stanzas v to viii Wordsworth seeks to explain the reasons for the loss of the 'visionary gleam'. He does this by proposing a view of human growth which resembles in certain respects ideas we have encountered previously (in poems such as 'Tintern Abbey', 'There was a boy' and 'To the Cuckoo') but is notably more pessimistic. The notion of pre-existence outlined at the beginning of stanza v is certainly new; and Wordsworth, reacting to criticism that he had sought to promote belief in a non-Christian doctrine, later insisted (in a note dictated to Isabella Fenwick) that he had not been arguing for philosophical acceptance of the concept but had borrowed the idea in order to make 'the best use of it I could as a Poet'. His primary concern is to suggest the erosion of the visionary power that occurs with the passing of time, and the myth of a prior state of existence, the memory of which steadily diminishes from the time of our birth, helps him to do this. The infant still feels close to the eternal source of life and can sense its presence all around him: 'Heaven lies about us in our infancy!' As his consciousness of his body's finite, material existence grows, however, his awareness of the eternal decreases and 'Shades of the prison-house begin to close/ Upon the growing Boy.' The child's insight into the reality of the natural world is still available, albeit in a weakened form, to the youth, described by Wordsworth as 'Nature's Priest'. But the visionary power dies with adulthood. The 'celestial light' or 'visionary gleam', which testifies to the existence of a radiant inner life, is obscured and eventually replaced by a different kind of light, that of ordinary material reality ('the light of common day'). Nature in fact assists this process, by encouraging the growing child to take delight in natural objects for their own sake rather than respond to their inner reality (stanza vi). Absorbed by sensory pleasure, the boy gradually forgets 'the glories he hath known'.

Stanza vii describes how the child begins at an early age to be engrossed in the trivialities of everyday existence. Eager to participate in what Wordsworth calls in 'Tintern Abbey' 'The dreary intercourse of daily life', the child practises his future roles at weddings and funerals and learns the language of business, love and strife. In comparing the child to an actor (l. 103) Wordsworth suggests how he imitates his elders but also implies that he betrays his true self. His involvement in the empty, superficial activities of daily living increase his remoteness from the source of existence, the 'home' (l. 65) where he belongs. The eighth stanza directly addresses the six-year-old child who was the subject of stanza vii (it is thought that Wordsworth had Coleridge's son Hartley in mind). The child is referred to as the 'best Philosopher' not because he has prodigious reasoning power and is capable of complex intellectual argument (in fact he is 'deaf and silent') but because he knows intuitively the truth that adult thinkers, whose responsiveness to reality has been deadened by the passage of time, labour to discover. The child's effortless insight into the essential life of things makes him an 'Eye among the blind'. Ironically, however, the child is unaware of the preciousness of his gift and is eager to participate in adult life, ignorant of 'the inevitable yoke' placed upon him by the passing years. The closing lines of the stanza vividly suggest how the child's vision will be increasingly suppressed by the dull repetitiveness of daily life:

> *Full soon thy Soul shall have her earthly freight,*
> *And custom lie upon thee with a weight,*
> *Heavy as frost, and deep almost as life!*

In the final stanzas of the poem (ix to xi) Wordsworth attempts to come to terms with his loss and considers what is left to sustain the adult. Firstly, the ability to remember childhood experiences means that those experiences are not lost to him but can still exercise an active influence on his perception. If he is unable to feel directly what he felt, then his memory at least makes available to him something akin to the childhood vision. Wordsworth finds this an abiding source of consolation:

> *The thought of our past years in me doth breed*
> *Perpetual benediction . . .*

He then elaborates on the most valuable aspects of his childhood experience. He gives thanks for

> *those obstinate questionings*
> *Of sense and outward things,*
> *Fallings from us, vanishings . . .*

Wordsworth seems here to be describing his obstinate refusal as a child to accept material reality. Material objects 'vanished' in that they were not felt to have an independent physical existence; rather, the child's oneness with nature was such that the objects were felt to be inseparable from his own being. In the Isabella Fenwick note referred to earlier Wordsworth gave a vivid account of this kind of experience:

I was often unable to think of external things as having external existence, and I communed with all that I saw as something not apart from, but inherent in, my own immaterial nature. Many times while going to school have I grasped at a wall or tree to recall myself from this abyss of idealism to the reality. At that time I was afraid of such processes. In later periods of life I have deplored, as we have all reason to do, a subjugation of an opposite character, and have rejoiced over the remembrances.

In the Ode these 'remembrances' are described as

> *shadowy recollections,*
> *Which, be they what they may,*
> *Are yet the fountain light of all our day,*
> *Are yet a master light of all our seeing . . .*

The insights of childhood can never again be directly experienced, but our memory of them affects our perception of the world and gives us lasting proof of an eternal reality. At the close of the stanza Wordsworth develops further the metaphor introduced in stanza v comparing human development to a journey away from the source of life. Although as adults we are 'inland', remote from 'that immortal sea', our recollections of past experience enable us to travel back and 'see the Children sport upon the shore,/ And hear the mighty waters rolling evermore'.

Stanza x returns to the exuberant natural scene described in stanzas iii and iv. Wordsworth is able now to share in the joy from which he had earlier felt excluded. However, the child's spontaneous, unthinking involvement in the life of nature is no longer possible. Man's unity with the natural world is not intuitively felt, but perceived as an intellectual truth: 'We in thought will join your throng'. Recognition of what has been lost is coupled with a determination to find comfort in the consolations of adulthood:

> *What though the radiance which was once so bright*
> *Be now for ever taken from my sight,*
> > *Though nothing can bring back the hour*
> *Of splendour in the grass, of glory in the flower;*
> > *We will grieve not, rather find*
> > *Strength in what remains behind . . .*

These consolations are enumerated in the remainder of the stanza. Firstly, there is 'the primal sympathy/ Which having been must ever be.' The feeling of kinship with the natural world which is one of the blessings of childhood is never completely destroyed but continues to exist in the memory. Secondly, there are 'the soothing thoughts that spring/ Out of human suffering'. Adulthood is characterized by an increased consciousness of, and sympathy for, one's fellow human beings (this idea was also present in 'Tintern Abbey', where Wordsworth observed that since his youth he had become aware of 'The still, sad music of humanity'). The reference to 'soothing thoughts' suggests also that the contemplation of suffering leads to the reassuring knowledge that human beings are not only linked to each other but also intimately connected to a larger reality. Finally, Wordsworth mentions 'the faith that looks through death' and 'the philosophic mind'. The child does not recognize his own mortality (in the Fenwick note Wordsworth recalled that 'Nothing was more difficult for me in childhood than to admit the notion of death as a state applicable to my own being'). The adult is more conscious of the fact of death, but his faith in the existence of an eternal reality, from which he came and to which he will eventually return, enables him to look beyond (or 'through') death. The quiet, meditative response to life that the adult alone is capable of is summed up in the expression 'the philosophic mind'.

The final stanza confirms Wordsworth's resolution of the problem he faced at the beginning of the poem. His response to the natural world has changed since childhood, but his love of nature is undiminished (indeed he believes it is now even greater), and the adult response offers its own kind of satisfaction:

> *I only have relinquished one delight*
> *To live beneath your more habitual sway.*

He reiterates that what he has gained is a new sensitivity to the mortality and suffering of his fellow human beings. This quality of tender sympathy is evident in the poem's closing lines:

> *To me the meanest flower that blows can give*
> *Thoughts that do often lie too deep for tears.*

The thoughts that are 'too deep for tears' seem also to be thoughts that can conquer grief. If through contemplation of natural objects we can make contact with the essential life of things, distress at the amount of pain in the world is replaced by a profounder sense of harmony and peace.

'Ode to Duty' and 'Elegiac Stanzas Suggested by a Picture of Peele Castle'

In the Immortality Ode, Wordsworth recognizes the decline of his visionary awareness and expresses a stoic determination to find strength in 'what remains behind'. The change that is explained and justified in the Ode is confirmed by other poems of the period, particularly in the 'Ode to Duty' (most of which is thought to have been written in 1804, the year Wordsworth finished the Immortality Ode) and 'Elegiac Stanzas' (probably 1806).

In the 'Ode to Duty' Wordsworth again bids farewell to the unthinking spontaneity of earlier years and welcomes in its place a conscious dedication to the virtues of reason and self-discipline. He can no longer identify with those who have an intuitive understanding of their own place in the world, and therefore of how to act in it:

> *There are who ask not if thine eye*
> *Be on them; who, in love and truth,*
> *Where no misgiving is, rely*
> *Upon the genial sense of youth:*
> *Glad hearts! without reproach or blot;*
> *Who do thy work, and know it not ...*

The instinctive responses of youth were no longer available to him, and he felt that his actions must henceforth be consciously determined. The above lines suggest a feeling of loss, but later in the poem there is a desire to escape the turbulence and intensity of his earlier experiences and a longing for serenity and order (there is a parallel here with the need to overcome emotional instability expressed in 'Resolution and

Independence'); 'Me this unchartered freedom tires ... I long for a repose that ever is the same.' The need for discipline and control in his personal life is reflected in the political and religious conservatism of Wordsworth's later years. His attainment of 'a repose that ever is the same' was also accompanied by an inevitable decline in the urgency and vitality of his poetry. F. R. Leavis comments that 'The Wordsworth who in the "Ode to Duty" spoke of the "genial sense of youth" as something he happily surrendered had seen the hiding-places of his power close.'

The change that Wordsworth underwent in this period was accelerated by the shattering impact of the death of his brother John, who drowned in February 1805. 'Elegiac Stanzas' alludes to this event when it speaks of a 'deep distress' which 'hath humanized my Soul' (l. 36). Peele Castle is close to Barrow-in-Furness in Cumbria, and Wordsworth had stayed near by in 1794. In 1806 he visited Sir George Beaumont and saw his painting of the castle. The poem depicts the shift in Wordsworth's attitudes to life by comparing his original impressions of the castle with his response twelve years later to Beaumont's painting.

Wordsworth first knew the castle during four weeks of calm summer weather. The first eight stanzas recall this time and evoke a scene of blissful harmony and tranquillity. The reflection of the castle was 'sleeping on a glassy sea', the sky was 'pure' and the air 'quiet'. If he had been a painter, Wordsworth tells us, he would have pictured this 'lasting ease' and added something else:

> the gleam,
> *The light that never was, on sea or land,*
> *The consecration, and the Poet's dream ...*

Wordsworth is clearly speaking again of the 'visionary gleam' and 'celestial light' referred to in the Immortality Ode. However, whereas the latter poem celebrated the visionary power of childhood and youth and lamented its passing, 'Elegiac Stanzas' appears to see the youthful conception of reality as deluded ('The light that never was ... the Poet's dream'). To his younger self the scene had a quality of eternal peace, but he now regards this as a 'fond illusion'. Nevertheless, there is still an element of regret in the recognition that the natural world can no longer be transfigured by his imagination. 'The light that never was' suggests not only naïve idealism but also the young Wordsworth's ability to perceive nature as something more than itself and so to 'consecrate' it. The poem as a whole asserts what has been gained from the experiences of maturity (in particular, from the death of his brother), but there has been loss as well: 'A power is gone, which nothing can restore.'

The second half of the poem (ll. 33–60) presents the changed outlook of the older Wordsworth. The distress of his brother's death 'hath humanized my Soul'. Belief in the value of solitary experience has been replaced by a desire to participate in the common life of humanity:

> *Farewell, farewell the heart that lives alone,*
> *Housed in a dream, at distance from the Kind!*

Before, he led an enclosed existence, shut off from his fellows ('Housed in a dream'). If he was aware of human suffering he had observed it from a distance; now his own experience of suffering has brought him closer to others. He admires Beaumont's painting because it is closer to the reality of life than his youthful illusions were. Beaumont pictured a castle lashed by heavy seas and battered by fierce winds. Its resolute defiance of the elements makes it an edifying example of strength in the face of adversity:

> *I love to see the look with which it braves,*
> *Cased in the unfeeling armour of old time,*
> *The lightning, the fierce wind, and trampling waves.*

Wordsworth himself wishes to endure life with a similar 'fortitude, and patient cheer'. Exposure to further suffering is actually to be welcomed because it will remind him of the true nature of human life; he therefore desires 'frequent sights of what is to be borne'. The final line, with its implied reference to an afterlife, suggests that solace is to be found in religious faith: 'Not without hope we suffer and we mourn.'

5. 'The Prelude'

An account of the origin and development of 'The Prelude' was given in Chapter 1. This chapter will look at the 1805 version of the poem more closely. Since a detailed analysis of the entire poem is impractical in a study-guide of this length, a general description of its overall structure and theme will be followed by an examination of a selection of significant and representative passages.

In 'The Prelude' Wordsworth traces his own development as a poet. This entails a search for the roots of his creative power, which he finds in the experiences of childhood. In particular, he concentrates in the early part of the poem upon the role of nature in shaping and stimulating his growing imagination. After describing various phases of adult experience he then returns to nature, which is recognized as an enduring source of strength, inspiration and renewal. Although the poem follows a broadly chronological sequence its shape is determined by the pattern of the poet's moral and spiritual growth rather than by the course of external events. The later books contain many references back to childhood, as when a moment of 'visionary dreariness' experienced at the age of five is recalled in Book XI because it illustrates Wordsworth's notion of 'spots of time', which remain with us and by which our adult minds are 'nourish'd and invisibly repair'd'. A general impression of the sequence of the poem can be gained from the titles of the books. The first four follow Wordsworth's life from infancy through schooldays to his time as a student at Cambridge and his final summer vacation. In the fifth book there is a pause in the narrative as Wordsworth reflects upon his early debt to reading. Books VI and VII cover his walking holiday in the Alps and later residence in London. Book VIII surveys retrospectively the way in which 'love of nature' led to 'love of mankind'. The next two books resume the narrative and describe Wordsworth's experience of the French Revolution. The last three books trace his spiritual recovery after the disillusionment that followed his return from France, and give thanks to nature, his wife, his sister Dorothy and Coleridge.

Introduction (Book I, ll. 1–304)

The exultant first verse paragraph of 'The Prelude' (ll. 1–30) celebrates the poet's freedom from the constrictions of city life. In the city he had been like a 'captive . . . immured' in a 'prison', but now he has emerged from his 'house/ Of bondage' and returned to the liberating spaciousness of nature. A refreshing breeze blows against his cheek 'from the green fields and from the clouds/ And from the sky'. As becomes clear in the next verse paragraph, this external wind parallels an inner 'creative breeze'; released from the city, Wordsworth experiences a revival of poetic inspiration. There is a similar correspondence between his speculation over which direction his journey from the city should take ('What dwelling shall receive me?') and his subsequent search for a theme for his poem. The description of the absolute freedom of choice enjoyed by the poet – 'The earth is all before me' – is a deliberate allusion to Adam and Eve's expulsion from the Garden of Eden in *Paradise Lost*:

> *The World was all before them, where to choose*
> *Their place of rest, and Providence their guide.*

However, Milton's lines come at the conclusion of his poem, and Adam and Eve have left Paradise behind them; the euphoric opening of 'The Prelude' suggests that Wordsworth's own paradise lies ahead of him. The journey in pursuit of a poetic theme will become a journey through time, and by the exercise of imagination and memory he will recover the lost paradise of childhood. Echoes of Milton are frequent in 'The Prelude', and later in Book I (ll. 179–80) Wordsworth explicitly considers making use of the kind of subject-matter associated with him. The parallels suggest that Wordsworth wished his work to have the weight and profundity of Milton's epic poetry but, as this first instance demonstrates, they also highlight marked differences in intention and method.

In determining the direction he should follow, Wordsworth as traveller and as poet is happy to be guided by nature:

> *I look about, and should the guide I chuse*
> *Be nothing better than a wandering cloud,*
> *I cannot miss my way.*
>
> *Or shall a twig, or any floating thing*
> *Upon the river, point me out my course?*

In the second verse paragraph (ll. 33–54) Wordsworth's future course begins to be more clearly defined. There is to be a disciplined commitment to 'chosen tasks' and he looks forward to 'active days'. That he is referring here to poetic creation is confirmed by the image of a 'mild, creative breeze',

> *A vital breeze which travell'd gently on*
> *O'er things which it had made, and is become*

> *A tempest, a redundant energy*
> *Vexing its own creation.*

Wordsworth explicitly parallels this inner stirring of inspiration and the 'sweet breath of Heaven' which blows against his body. As has been seen in our readings of other poems, imagery which is expressive of a correspondence between man and nature is characteristic of Wordsworth. His development of the image, with the 'breeze' turning into a 'tempest', suggests how the surge of inspiration becomes uncontrolled and over-powering; his creative energy is excessive to the point where it is felt to be self-defeating and to frustrate poetic composition. Nevertheless, like a storm 'breaking up a long-continued frost', the return of inspiration promises to revive the poet and stimulate new creative achievements.

The poem now moves forward in time, and Wordsworth comments retrospectively on the spontaneity of the previous lines (ll. 55–67). He is not used to making 'A present joy the matter of my Song' but recalls that he was able to 'Pour out, that day, my soul in measur'd strains'. The rush of inspiration had encouraged him to believe that he had been 'singled out' to create a momentous work of poetry: 'great hopes were mine'. Feeling a 'chearful confidence in things to come' he had then rested at a 'green shady place' and deliberately allowed his thoughts to slacken (ll. 68–94). Wordsworth is continuing to use the metaphor of a journey to represent the process of poetic creation; just as the traveller had become more sure of his eventual destination ('I made a choice/ Of one sweet Vale whither my steps should turn'), so the poet was confident that he was about to begin 'some work/ Of glory'. Appropriately, the resumption of his journey was accompanied by an attempt to reawaken the creative inspiration he had earlier felt (ll. 95–115). On this occasion, however, the 'creative breeze' flagged and eventually ceased altogether. His soul did not lack 'Eolian visitations', but

> *the harp*
> *Was soon defrauded, and the banded host*
> *Of harmony dispers'd in straggling sounds*
> *And, lastly, utter silence.*

(The Aeolian harp produces sounds when the wind passes over its strings and was used by other Romantic poets as a symbol of poetic inspiration.) Far from feeling dispirited by the slackening of his creative energy Wordsworth accepted it as fit and proper:

> *'Be it so,*
> *It is an injury,' said I, 'to this day*
> *To think of any thing but present joy.'*

79

He was happy to give himself over to direct enjoyment of nature ('It was a splendid evening'). To attempt to transform experience into poetry would, on this day at least, have been both unnecessary ('What need of many words?') and inhibiting; he had no desire to 'bend the sabbath of that time/ To a servile yoke'. While poetic activity had earlier been compared to 'holy services' (l. 63), Wordsworth now considered it sacrilegious to seek to impose language and form on the splendours of nature.

The creative urge soon returned, however, though inspiration remained elusive (ll. 116–41). The traveller had arrived at his 'hermitage' but the poet had yet to locate his theme. Nevertheless, the desire to create now had a pressing urgency ('speedily a longing in me rose/ To brace myself to some determin'd aim'). He decided to devote himself to 'reading or thinking', preparing for the task ahead by collecting together new material or (more significantly) contemplating his past life in order to 'rescue from decay' old experiences. Wordsworth now returns to the present, and reports that although he would 'gladly grapple with some noble theme' inspiration has again faltered:

> But I have been discouraged; gleams of light
> Flash often from the East, then disappear
> And mock me with a sky that ripens not
> Into a steady morning . . .

The poet then says that it would bring him contentment if he could put aside his 'lofty hopes' and be satisfied by less ambitious works (ll. 142–4). His restlessness and frustration cannot be so easily shaken off, however (ll. 144–56). He analyses his own fitness for the creation of a 'glorious work' and finds that 'the report/ Is often cheering' (ll. 157–70). He has 'the vital soul' (imagination), understanding of general philosophical truths and a store of 'external things,/ Forms, images' (this probably refers principally to his memories of natural objects). This account of the resources necessary to a poet emphasizes the role of the poet's own creative power. The 'vital soul' is the 'first great gift', while objective philosophical truths are merely 'subordinate helpers of the living mind'. His difficulty is deciding upon a subject for his poem (ll. 170–251). He considers at some length writing a traditional epic, and mentions various heroic figures who might warrant such treatment. However, Wordsworth says he lacks the confidence to tackle such subject-matter. In any case, his greatest yearning is to produce 'some philosophic Song/ Of Truth that cherishes our daily life' (ll. 231–2). But this too appears an 'awful burthen', and he tells himself that such a project should wait until he has developed a 'riper mind' and 'clearer insight' – though he is aware that this may simply be an excuse to justify his inactivity.

The poet is again tempted to abandon 'zeal' and 'ambition' and settle back into a relaxed enjoyment of nature (ll. 252–71). But the longing for creative fulfilment reasserts itself; he realizes that if he gave himself over to 'listlessness' he would be

> *Unprofitably travelling towards the grave,*
> *Like a false steward who hath much received*
> *And renders nothing back.*

These lines confirm that the poet's journey is not yet over, but one possible route is here eliminated. He knows he has an obligation to use his poetic gift. And then, as he deliberately turns away from this 'unprofitable' path, he suddenly finds his journey's end:

> *Was it for this*
> *That one, the fairest of all Rivers, lov'd*
> *To blend his murmurs with my Nurse's song,*
> *And from his alder shades and rocky falls,*
> *And from his fords and shallows, sent a voice*
> *That flow'd along my dreams?*

ll. 271–6

Wordsworth recollects his childhood self in order to confirm that nature from his earliest years had singled him out to be a poet, but in doing so he has found his subject: the growth of a poet's mind. The poem that follows is ostensibly an attempt to rouse himself from his lethargy by tracing the development of his poetic power. It is therefore to be a poem of autobiographical exploration rather than a conventional epic or the 'philosophical poem' that Wordsworth earlier declared to be his 'last and favourite inspiration' (that poem was intended to be 'The Recluse', to which 'The Prelude' was, according to the Preface to 'The Excursion', 'preparatory' and 'subsidiary'). In suggesting that the natural world communicated with the young Wordsworth ('sent a voice'), this first reference to childhood establishes the recurrent theme of the first two books of 'The Prelude'. The river (identified in line 277 as the Derwent) ordered Wordsworth's knowledge and perception of reality ('compos'd my thoughts/ To more than infant softness'), giving him an intimation of the essential harmony and tranquillity of nature ('the calm/ Which Nature breathes among the hills and groves'). The poet then recalls bathing in a tributary of the river when a five-year-old boy (ll. 286–304).

It was a period of rapturous absorption in the physical pleasures offered by nature; he 'Bask'd in the sun, and plunged, and bask'd again . . . or cours'd/ Over the sandy fields, leaping through groves/ Of yellow grunsel.' The child's immersion in the stream suggests that his experiences were a kind of baptism, initiating him into a life that was to be intimately connected with nature.

Robbing snares, the raven's nest and the stolen boat (Book I, ll. 305–50 and 373–427)

In the first two books of 'The Prelude' Wordsworth describes how during his childhood the simple physical enjoyment of nature was gradually replaced by a response to the natural world that was more spiritual and more conscious. He began to be aware of hidden forces at work within nature, and of the complex ways in which humanity is related to the non-human universe. His experiences of nature, whether joyful or unsettling, moulded his character:

> *Fair seed-time had my soul, and I grew up*
> *Foster'd alike by beauty and by fear . . .*

Book I, ll. 305–6

The three episodes that will now be discussed are examples of nature's 'ministry'.

The three episodes have a pattern that is to recur in 'The Prelude'. Wordsworth describes an incident and then recollects the imaginative insight that it induced. The first involves the trapping of woodcocks in snares. It occurs a few years later than his innocent bathing in the River Derwent ('ere I had seen/ Nine summers'), and his relationship with nature has become more self-conscious and as a consequence more troubled. Although he commits wrong by robbing other boys' snares, his uneasiness stems not only from the knowledge that he is guilty of theft. The trapping of the birds is in itself destructive of nature (he describes himself as a 'fell destroyer'), and his very presence, as a human being now conscious of his own independent existence, seems a further violation of nature's peace:

> *moon and stars*
> *Were shining o'er my head; I was alone,*
> *And seem'd to be a trouble to the peace*
> *That was among them.*

The stealing of birds trapped by others (which he certainly knew to be wrong: 'a strong desire/ O'er power'd my better reason') simply adds to the burden of guilt already oppressing him. The sounds of pursuit he believes he can hear after carrying out the theft ('I heard among the solitary hills/ Low breathings coming after me') are partly a projection of this guilt. The boy is conscious of having violated nature, and he imagines nature expressing its disapproval both of this and of his theft. The 'low breathings' and quiet footsteps are, viewed in this light, sounds made by the boy himself. In appearing to confirm his guilt the landscape thus has a moral influence upon the child. At the same time, however, the boy is responding to a secret, mysterious life that not only exists in his imagination but is actually there in nature. Such experiences, in which Wordsworth communed with an invisible life force, were amongst the most profound and formative of his childhood.

In the bird-nesting episode we again find the young Wordsworth engaged in an activity which he knows to be illicit but which has consequences that are felt to be beneficial. His object was 'mean' and 'inglorious', yet 'the end/ Was not ignoble'. Bent on a wilful act of violence against nature, he is a 'plunderer' whose presence on the mountains disturbs nature's tranquillity. As he hangs precariously on the rock-face, however, the secret life of nature is again revealed to him. Natural objects take on a changed identity; the sound of the wind was a 'strange utterance', the sky 'seem'd not a sky/ Of earth' and 'with what motion mov'd the clouds!' The boy's altered perception of his surroundings is partly explained by simple giddiness, but he is also briefly aware – though the experience is imperfectly understood – of nature's inner reality.

Although these experiences were unnerving, they were nevertheless instances of nature's 'ministry' (l. 370). In retrospect Wordsworth sees that nature was exercising a beneficent influence on the growth of his consciousness. This ministry was sometimes gentle (l. 367) but could also take a 'severer' form (l. 370). Another example of the latter is the famous boat-stealing episode. Wordsworth describes taking a shepherd's boat and rowing it out on to a lake. As he travels away from the cave where the boat had been moored, he feels a sense of guilt but is also exhilarated. It was 'an act of stealth/ And troubled pleasure', but he is proud of his skill (l. 396) and with enthusiasm pulled 'lustily' on the oars. The episode appeals to the boy's sense of adventure and he has a romantic conception of his boat being an 'elfin pinnace'. The forceful movement of the boat, which 'Went heaving through the water, like a Swan', reflects his elation and self-confidence. Suddenly, however, the boy becomes the victim of an optical illusion which thoroughly unsettles him:

> *from behind that craggy Steep, till then*
> *The bound of the horizon, a huge Cliff,*
> *As if with voluntary power instinct,*
> *Uprear'd its head.*

When he rowed away from the cave the boy had fixed his gaze upon the top of a ridge, behind which there initially seemed to be nothing but the sky. As he rowed further out on to the lake, however, a more distinct peak, behind the ridge, came into view. The further he is from the shore (and his first instinct is to row faster: 'I struck, and struck again') the more he can see of the mountain; it therefore seemed to be 'growing still in stature'. There is, then, an extremely rational explanation for what the boy sees. His imagination, however, transforms the mountain into a 'living thing' which 'strode after me'.

This image of a monstrous figure which 'Uprear'd its head' and then pursued the terrified Wordsworth reminds us of the giants to be found in children's story-books. The episode thus illustrates vividly a typical fear of childhood. At the same time the pursuing mountain, like the 'low breathings' he heard after robbing the snares, is a projection of the boy's guilt. He knows he has done wrong and imagines nature admonishing him for his crime. But in the days that followed, the incident took on a more profound significance:

> *after I had seen*
> *That spectacle, for many days, my brain*
> *Work'd with a dim and undetermin'd sense*
> *Of unknown modes of being; in my thoughts*
> *There was a darkness, call it solitude,*
> *Or blank desertion, no familiar shapes*
> *Of hourly objects, images of trees,*
> *Of sea or sky, no colours of green fields;*
> *But huge and mighty Forms that do not live*
> *Like living men mov'd slowly through my mind*
> *By day and were the trouble of my dreams.*

Wordsworth's language here acknowledges the difficulty of defining what it was that he experienced. His willingness to use expressions such as 'undetermin'd', 'unknown' and 'call it solitude' indicates his intellectual honesty. The experience appears to have involved a new insight into the reality of the world about him. Rather than picturing in his mind the familiar external forms of nature, he had a 'dim' sense of a universe governed by vast and mysterious forces. The boy was also learning about his own imaginative power. His mind worked on what had taken place in the boat and this enabled him to experience new kinds of awareness.

'Bless'd the infant Babe' (Book II, ll. 237–80)

In the first two books of 'The Prelude' Wordsworth's attempt to determine the factors which influence the growth of the human consciousness mostly takes the form of recollecting significant experiences in his own childhood. This next passage is less specifically autobiographical and traces the origins of human perception back still further, to the earliest months of life. A baby who experiences a mother's love is initiated into loving relationships with other human beings and encouraged also to feel that he is intimately connected with the external world. Soon after birth the baby instinctively desires to attach himself to a fellow human being ('Claims manifest kindred with an earthly soul') and responds eagerly to the physical and emotional expressions of his mother's love ('Nurs'd in his Mother's arms ... sleeps/ Upon his Mother's breast ... Doth gather passion from his Mother's eye'). The love he receives stimulates his spiritual growth, passing into his 'torpid life' like an 'awakening breeze' (the image is similar to that of the 'creative breeze' which revived Wordsworth's poetic imagination at the beginning of the poem). The child's perception of his mother as a being who is at once outside himself and inseparably connected to him leads him to a similar perception of external objects. He develops the ability to organize his initially disparate visual impressions, arranging the elements of the material world into unified and coherent wholes:

> eager to combine
> In one appearance, all the elements
> And parts of the same object, else detach'd
> And loth to coalesce.

All of the child's perceptions are influenced by the consciousness of his mother's love. He senses her 'beloved Presence' in all things. She is therefore the source of

> A virtue which irradiates and exalts
> All objects through all objects of sense.

F. R. Leavis noted the similarity between these lines and a famous passage in 'Tintern Abbey':

> *A motion and a spirit, that impels*
> *All thinking things, all objects of all thought,*
> *And rolls through all things.*

The child's sense of a world unified by his mother's pervasive presence anticipates (is indeed the necessary prelude to) the adult's visionary experience of an inner life force that permeates and 'impels' the universe. The child feels that the objects of the material world are connected not only to each other but also to him. The close, loving relationship with his mother develops into a broader sense of affinity with his sur-roundings:

> *No outcast he, bewilder'd and depress'd;*
> *Along his infant veins are interfus'd*
> *The gravitation and the filial bond*
> *Of nature, that connect him with the world.*

There is a natural force (a 'gravitation') which attracts the child to the world outside himself and encourages him to feel part of it, and this is reinforced by the 'filial bond' between mother and baby, which is itself an expression of the larger bond between humanity and nature. The child knows that he belongs in the world, but he is not just a passive inhabitant; 'Emphatically such a Being lives', and he is 'An inmate of this *active* universe'. The child's mind interacts with external objects, and through the exercise of his imaginative power he arrives at his own conception of reality. His mind is therefore 'creator and receiver both' and works 'in alliance with the works/ Which it beholds'.

Wordsworth calls this active imaginative response to the world a 'Poetic spirit'. With most people it is eroded in later years but for some (who are, by implication, poets) it remains 'Pre-eminent till death'. The decline of visionary power was a theme Wordsworth returned to in the Immortality Ode, though in that poem (written five years after these lines, which originally appeared in the two-part 'Prelude' of 1799) he is less confident about his ability as a poet to retain the insights of childhood and advances a philosophy of early human growth that is markedly less optimistic.

The discharged soldier (Book IV, ll. 363–504)

The discharged soldier can be grouped with the solitary figures found elsewhere in Wordsworth's poems (examples discussed in previous chapters include the Old Cumberland Beggar and the leech-gatherer in 'Resolution and Independence'). Like most of the other solitaries the discharged soldier responds to his hardship with an attitude of stoic acceptance. Another common factor is the profound influence the soldier and the other solitaries have upon Wordsworth; the descriptions of his meetings with these strange, compelling figures frequently carry suggestions of visionary experience.

The encounter with the soldier occurs when Wordsworth is walking alone at night along a moonlit road. The setting (ll. 363–99) is one of absolute tranquillity; the road is 'deserted', and its 'watery surface . . . glittered in the moon' and seemed to Wordsworth 'another stream/ Creeping with silent lapse to join the brook/ That murmur'd in the valley'. Wordsworth himself is 'listless' and 'quiescent', occasionally conscious of his immediate surroundings but oblivious of any more distant prospect. He is in a trance-like state, the stillness of the scene having a restorative effect that is 'Like the calm of sleep,/ But sweeter far'. His sense of blissful accord with nature is such that the impressions he receives from without seem like creations of his own imagination:

> *O happy state! what beauteous pictures now*
> *Rose in harmonious imagery – they rose*
> *As from some distant region of my soul*
> *And came along like dreams.*

Wordsworth's reverie is dramatically interrupted when another person suddenly appears on the road. The flow of soothing, harmonious images comes to an abrupt halt as he reaches a turning in the road and sees an 'uncouth shape' (l. 402). The figure is recognizably human, 'of stature tall' and 'clad in military garb'; and his 'murmuring sounds', which suggest some kind of pain or uneasiness, are in contrast to the tranquil murmuring of the brook. But at the same time (and this is a recurring characteristic of Wordsworth's solitaries) there is much about him that seems to border on the inanimate. In particular, he has an eerie stillness: 'his form/ Kept the same stillness . . . at his feet/ His shadow lay, and mov'd not . . . he remain'd/ Fix'd to his place.' The suggestion that he is barely human is enhanced by his spectral quality; his mouth 'Shew'd ghastly in the moonlight', and Wordsworth beholds with 'astonishment' his 'ghastly figure' and later he shows 'the same ghastly mildness in his look'. Wordsworth seems almost to be experiencing a supernatural visitation (there is a similar suggestion in 'Resolution and Independence', where he speculates that the encounter with the leech-gatherer is a 'leading from above'). The man tells Wordsworth that he has served abroad as a soldier but has now been dismissed. His distressed circumstances reinforce the idea that he is outside the mainstream of human society.

The appearance of the soldier startles Wordsworth out of his mood of relaxed, solitary contemplation and reawakens his social self, reminding him of the responsibility he has towards his fellow human beings. It is Wordsworth who makes the first attempt at contact, leaving the hiding-place from where he has been observing the soldier and raising his arm in welcome. The gesture brings a response (he 'Return'd my salutation'), and it is as if the soldier is gradually coming to life, re-entering, with Wordsworth's assistance, the human domain. The process continues as Wordsworth engages the man in conversation, asking him his history. When he hears of the hardship the soldier has suffered he determines to find him shelter for the night. He is confident that a labourer who lives near by will provide him with food and lodging. They reach the labourer's cottage, and Wordsworth prepares to bid the man farewell. In describing the end of their encounter he refers to the soldier as his 'Comrade', suggesting that his compassion has brought the two men closer together. Confirmation that the soldier has been rescued from his isolation and brought back into the human community is provided by his thanking Wordsworth 'with a reviving interest,/ Till then unfelt'.

Although the soldier's mysterious calmness had unsettled Wordsworth, it denotes an imperviousness to suffering which is impressive as well as unnerving. This awesome composure is evident in his manner when speaking of his misfortunes. He tells his story 'with a quiet, uncomplaining voice,/ A stately air of mild indifference'. When questioned further he retains his 'demeanour calm', and Wordsworth notes that

> in all he said
> *There was a strange half-absence, and a tone*
> *Of weakness and indifference, as of one*
> *Remembering the importance of his theme*
> *But feeling it no longer.*

Like the leech-gatherer, the soldier is an example to Wordsworth of human fortitude. He is sustained by a quiet faith in God and the goodness of humanity; advised that in future he should seek out help when in need of it, he replies:

> *'my trust is in the God of Heaven*
> *And in the eye of him that passes me'.*

Crossing the Alps (Book VI, ll. 488–572)

Wordsworth's description of his descent of the Simplon Pass and the invocation to imagination which precedes it are among the most celebrated passages of 'The Prelude'. Both are essential to an understanding of the belief, central in Wordsworth's poetry, that it is through the imagination that humanity is capable of apprehending its unity with the eternal life of nature. They are prefaced by a passage of straightforward narrative (ll. 488–524). Accompanied by a friend, Wordsworth is on a walking tour of France and Switzerland in 1790. Joining a party of travellers, the two companions set out to cross the Alps. When the party stops for lunch before commencing the eagerly anticipated final stage of the journey Wordsworth and his friend become separated from the others. They start to make the final ascent by themselves but become worried that they have lost their way. They seek directions from a peasant and are perplexed when instead of telling them how they can continue their upward climb he advises them on how to descend. Gradually it becomes clear to them that without realizing it they have in fact already crossed the Alps.

Although less memorable, this introductory passage is fundamentally related to what follows. The episode indicates that revelatory experience is unlikely to occur when consciously sought. It also suggests that another reason for Wordsworth's disappointment was that he was expecting inspiration to come exclusively from external stimuli. The spectacular scenery of the Alps had been celebrated by many eighteenth-century writers, and Wordsworth was clearly expecting to be profoundly impressed. However, the most deeply satisfying experiences of nature are unavailable to the passive recipient of sensory impressions. Landscape can have the kind of impact Wordsworth was seeking only when it is transformed by the inner power of the imagination.

It is to the imagination that Wordsworth, breaking off from his narrative, now turns (ll. 525–48). The onset of imaginative power described in this verse paragraph seems to have occurred during the moment of composition itself. The past tense of the opening lines might initially give the impression that imagination 'came/ Athwart' Wordsworth after speaking to the peasant; the present tense in ll. 531–2, however, indicates that the experience evoked is more immediate. As well as moving abruptly forward in time, the poem undergoes a dramatic change of tone as it switches from a straightforward recitation of external events to an impassioned celebration of inner creative power. It is imagination which reveals to us the invisible life of things:

> the light of sense
> Goes out in flashes that have shewn to us
> The invisible world.

'Goes out' here could mean 'is emitted' or 'is extinguished'. The ambiguity is appropriate because the response to the external world Wordsworth is seeking to define is initially dependent on the senses but then becomes something which transcends the sensory. The world is normally apprehended by the senses, but the moments of supreme vision occur when sight develops into insight; the '*invisible* world' is lit up and made visible, as if by a flash of light. When this perception of inner reality is experienced the normal operation of the senses is suspended; the 'light of sense' is therefore extinguished, and we become aware of an eternal life force, of 'infinitude' (l. 539).

The capacity of the imagination to apprehend the hidden life of natural landscape is now demonstrated in Wordsworth's account of his descent of the Simplon Pass (ll. 549–72). After the anticlimax of learning that they have crossed the Alps the downward journey of Wordsworth and his friend is at first a tedious one. Their pace slows down to a 'dull and heavy slackening'; then they enter the 'gloomy Pass' and travel for 'several hours/ At a slow step'. But the spectacular scenery eventually compels Wordsworth's attention. Although his ultimate perception is of a transcendent harmony, the details of the scene initially suggest confusion and disunity. The landscape is full of bewildering contradictions; the waterfalls, despite their powerful and incessant movement, seem static (they appear 'stationary blasts'); the woods are 'decaying', yet 'never to be decayed'. The elements of nature seem in conflict, with 'Winds thwarting winds' and 'torrents shooting from the clear blue sky'. In its response to the scene the human mind at first appears inadequate. The woods defy any attempt to impose graspable limits upon their size and are 'immeasurable'. The words 'sick', 'giddy' and 'raving' suggest not only the turbulence of the landscape but also the severe disorientation experienced by Wordsworth as he struggles to come to terms with that turbulence. But the characteristics of the scene which finally enable him to derive reassurance from it are in fact implicit in the very elements which initially induce fear and bafflement. Firstly, the unsettling turmoil of the landscape (the 'raving' stream, the 'unfetter'd clouds', the 'shooting' torrents) is proof of a dynamic and indestructible *life*. Secondly, nature has the power to convey its life to a human observer, and the human observer the power to receive the message and, eventually, understand it. Just as in the bird-nesting episode the young Wordsworth listened to the wind's 'Strange utterance', so here the sounds of the landscape are again described in a way which suggests meaningful communication:

> *The rocks that mutter'd close upon our ears,*
> *Black drizzling crags that spake by the way-side*
> *As if a voice were in them ...*

In the magnificent climax to the passage Wordsworth finally realizes that what the landscape expresses is nature's eternal life and ultimate unity. The diverse elements of the scene are at last perceived to be

> *like workings of one mind, the features*
> *Of the same face, blossoms upon one tree,*
> *Characters of the great Apocalypse,*
> *The types and symbols of Eternity,*
> *Of first and last, and midst, and without end.*

It is the imagination that enables Wordsworth's consciousness to break through the outward chaos of the scene and recognize that these external features are 'types' and 'symbols' of a deeper reality. In describing the scene as 'like workings of one mind' he is therefore not only saying that the entire landscape was an expression of the force which originated it, he is also acknowledging the part played by *his* mind in creating the landscape's unity. The passage is a superb example of the mind as

> *creator and receiver both,*
> *Working but in alliance with the works*
> *Which it beholds.*

Book II, ll. 273–5

This triumph of the imagination is all the more profoundly satisfying because it suggests that the mind is capable of perceiving the essential unity of the universe even when nature is encountered at its most bewilderingly diverse. 'Tumult and peace, the darkness and the light' can be reconciled and felt as one.

'Spots of time' (Book XI, ll. 258–389)

The notion of 'spots of time' is of crucial significance in Wordsworth's poetry and is particularly important to an understanding of 'The Prelude'. In this passage he begins by defining what he means by the expression and then illustrates the concept by recollecting two specific episodes from his childhood. 'Spots of time' are certain key experiences which remain within us as a resource from which we can obtain restoration and renewal. They have a 'vivifying Virtue' by means of which

> *our minds*
> *Are nourish'd and invisibly repair'd,*
> *A virtue by which pleasure is enhanced*
> *That penetrates, enables us to mount*
> *When high, more high, and lifts us up when fallen.*

When these experiences have occurred we have usually felt that 'the mind/ Is Lord and master, and that outward sense/ Is but the obedient servant of her will'. Our sensory faculties play a part in the experiences but they are subordinate to imaginative power. Again we see Wordsworth's belief that in its finest moments the mind is not a passive receiver of sense-impressions but makes an active response to the external world. He suggests that these spots of time are 'scatter'd everywhere' but are particularly to be found in childhood. (It is relevant here to recall that, in a note to the Immortality Ode, Wordsworth said that as a child his mind was sometimes so much the 'lord and master' of his senses that he would grasp at a wall or tree 'to recall myself from this abyss of idealism to the reality'.) Although the two incidents introduced by this passage are the only ones explicitly identified by Wordsworth as spots of time, it seems fair to apply the term to the poem's other episodes of imaginative intensity – such episodes as the robbing of snares, the stolen boat, the journey through the Simplon Pass and the ascent of Snowdon.

The first experience used by Wordsworth as an example of his concept occurred when he was five years old (ll. 279–326). He went riding on the moors near Penrith with a servant and became separated from him. He was frightened and his fear increased when, after dismounting from his horse, he came across the site of a gibbet where many years before a murderer had been hanged. Although little remained of the gibbet, the man's name inscribed in turf was a vivid reminder of the gruesome event. Wordsworth fled in terror and then encountered a scene which made an even greater impact upon him:

> *A naked Pool that lay beneath the hills,*
> *The Beacon on the summit, and more near,*
> *A Girl who bore a Pitcher on her head*
> *And seem'd with difficult steps to force her way*
> *Against the blowing wind.*

The scene was one of bleakness and desolation: the naked pool, the remote beacon, the lonely figure of the girl. Yet the memory of it became a source of pleasure and strength. The boy's imagination perceived the unity in the scene and enabled him to confer an emotional life on his surroundings, investing them with a 'visionary dreariness'. It is the knowledge of his own imaginative power that enables him in later years to derive joy and comfort from his memory of the experience. When he was courting Mary Hutchinson he frequently revisited the spot, and, because this was a 'blessed time of early love', it radiated 'The spirit of pleasure and youth's golden gleam'. But this pleasure was increased still further by the recollection of the earlier experience.

Before describing the second incident Wordsworth elaborates upon the significance and value of such spots of time (ll. 326–45). Memories of occasions in the past when the imagination was strong sustain us in the present ('diversity of strength/ Attends us, if but once we have been strong'). Again it is emphasized that our natures can be fulfilled only if our response to external stimuli is creative rather than passive ('from thyself it is that thou must give,/ Else never canst receive'). The formative experiences of childhood, when the imagination is particularly powerful, are thus the 'base' on which adult 'greatness' is built. At this point, however, the optimism of the passage suddenly falters. A sentence which begins as an apparently confident assertion of the continued availability to Wordsworth of his childhood experiences ends by emphasizing their elusiveness:

> The days gone by
> Come back upon me from the dawn almost
> Of life: the hiding-places of my power
> Seem open; I approach, and then they close;
> I see by glimpses now; when age comes on,
> May scarcely see at all . . .

The increasing difficulty of recollecting the thoughts and sensations of childhood is inevitably accompanied by a decline in visionary power – the ability to look at natural objects and, as in childhood, find them 'Apparelled in celestial light' (a quotation from the Immortality Ode, another poem which laments the fading of visionary insight). Wordsworth feels an urgent need to record, while he is able, such experiences from the past as he can still recall, in the hope that once preserved they will continue to be a source of regeneration. At the beginning of 'The Prelude' he had felt the desire to 'rescue from decay' past experiences (Book I, l. 126); here he expresses a similar intention:

> I would give,
> While yet we may, as far as words can give,
> A substance and a life to what I feel:
> I would enshrine the spirit of the past
> For future restoration.

He now recollects the second 'affecting incident', which took place when he was thirteen (ll. 345–89). At the end of a school term he climbed to the top of a crag and impatiently watched the two roads below, along either of which the horses that would take him home might travel. As in the previous spot of time, the scene is wild and desolate, though at the time the boy's attention was distracted from his surroundings by his mood of restless expectancy:

> 'twas a day
> Stormy, and rough, and wild, and on the grass
> I sate, half-shelter'd by a naked wall;
> Upon my right hand was a single sheep,
> · A whistling hawthorn on my left . . .

During the holidays, however, his father died, and this scene returned to him with renewed force. He felt overwhelming sadness and an obscure sense of guilt, and these emotions impressed themselves upon his memory of the melancholy landscape ('The single sheep, and the one blasted tree,/ And the bleak music of that old stone wall'). Again he had experienced the power of the imagination to invest natural objects with an added significance, and the episode is one to which his mind 'often would repair and thence would drink,/ As at a fountain'.

The ascent of Snowdon (Book XIII, ll. 1–116)

For a detailed discussion of this passage (the climax of 'The Prelude'), see the section on 'Imagination' in Chapter 7.

6. Later Poetry

Wordsworth completed 'The Prelude' in May 1805. With one or two exceptions, the poems for which he is usually remembered had all been written. Over the remaining forty-five years of his life his output continued to be prodigious, but the decline in quality is distressingly obvious. Some critics have praised the technical perfection of the later verse, but it is generally accepted that the energy and intensity of the great decade are missing.

The likely reasons for this deterioration can be gleaned from poems written during the crucial years of change. Firstly, there was the loss of visionary power, alluded to in 'The Prelude' ('the hiding-places of my power/ Seem open; I approach, and then they close') and explicitly lamented in the Immortality Ode, composed between 1802 and 1804. 'Elegiac Stanzas' (1806) actually welcomes the loss, dismissing the visionary experiences of earlier years as youthful illusion ('The light that never was'). Wordsworth's finest poetry vividly recreates moments of heightened awareness and insight, but these moments belonged mainly to youth and early manhood and became increasingly difficult to recover through recollection. 'Elegiac Stanzas' also records the devastating impact of the death of Wordsworth's brother, John, in 1805. Later (in 1812) he suffered the deaths of two of his children. Wordsworth had always been subject to emotional instability (as the opening verses of 'Resolution and Independence' demonstrate), and these events must have threatened his ability to maintain a secure hold on life. In the 'Ode to Duty' (1804–6) the poet longs for 'a repose that ever is the same', and in 'Elegiac Stanzas' Peele Castle is admired as an embodiment of fortitude and endurance. These two poems point towards the means by which Wordsworth withstood emotional upheaval and towards the recurring preoccupations of the later poetry. Instead of recollecting experiences of visionary insight the poems increasingly assert the value of such conventional virtues as order, resolution and duty. There is also a move towards orthodox Christianity, explained perhaps by the need to be sustained in his bereavement by belief in an afterlife. The world of Wordsworth's later poems is a public rather than a private one; we no longer feel that we are accompanying the poet on a courageous exploration of his inner life. This movement away from personal experience is seen at its worst in sonnets on such subjects as 'The Projected Kendal and Windermere Railway' and 'Illustrated Books and Newspapers'. Such poems are characterized not only by a triteness of subject-matter, but also by a sententious, moralizing tone and a depressing conventionality of attitude.

'The Excursion', published in 1814, is a more substantial achievement but nevertheless is far inferior to 'The Prelude' (both poems were intended to be part of 'The Recluse', the great philosophical work that Wordsworth never completed). Most of the poem was composed between 1809 and 1813 but some passages were written earlier. In particular, Book I contains 'The Ruined Cottage', written between 1795 and 1797 as a separate poem. Most of 'The Excursion' is taken up by a series of long speeches, linked by a minimal plot. The poet, accompanied by the Wanderer, a rural philosopher who derives strength from his closeness to the natural world, meets the Solitary, a disillusioned revolutionary who has lost his faith in human nature. The Wanderer seeks to overcome the Solitary's pessimism and is assisted by the Pastor, who stresses the virtues of Christianity. The three principal characters represent different aspects or phases of Wordsworth's own thought, but in externalizing the conflicts he has experienced Wordsworth deadens their impact; the poem lacks the urgency and conviction of 'The Prelude'. The narrative of 'The Ruined Cottage' is significantly by far the strongest part of the poem. Most of the rest is worthy but dull; the heavy-handed didacticism of much of the verse provoked Keats's famous objection to 'poetry that has a palpable design on us'.

'The White Doe of Rylstone', written in 1807 and published in 1815, again uses a fictional narrative to present Wordsworth's moral attitudes, but does so more successfully. The poem is set during the reign of Queen Elizabeth I. The heroine, Emily, suffers the destruction of her family in the course of a Catholic insurrection which she, as a Protestant, cannot support. The poem celebrates Emily's powers of endurance, which ultimately enable her to overcome despair:

> *Her duty is to stand and wait;*
> In resignation to abide
> The shock, AND FINALLY SECURE
> O'ER PAIN AND GRIEF A TRIUMPH PURE.

ll. 1069–72

(The italics and capitals are Wordsworth's own.) Emily is comforted through her ordeal by a white doe, which symbolizes the consolation that can be derived from patience and resolution. The animal helps Emily transcend her suffering; it is through the doe that she becomes aware of ultimate immortality. The creature's significance is stressed at the close of the poem:

> *'Thou, thou art not a Child of Time,*
> *But Daughter of the Eternal Prime!'*

ll. 1909–10

The Duddon sonnets, a series of poems written between 1806 and 1820, are also exceptions to the general mediocrity of the later years. Wordsworth follows the River Duddon from its source to the sea, each sonnet marking a different stage of the journey. In addition to tracing the changes in the river, the sequence of poems incorporates reflections upon the nature of human growth. There are several outstanding poems in the group, most notably 'Whence that low voice?' and the concluding sonnet, 'After-thought'.

Other poems that deserve mention are 'Extempore Effusion upon the Death of James Hogg' (1835) and 'Surprised by joy – impatient as the Wind' (1815), a moving sonnet inspired by the death of the poet's daughter in 1812. These and the other poems that have been referred to were, however, isolated achievements. It was perhaps inevitable that the remarkable creative intensity of the years before 1805 could not be sustained; certainly the poetry of those years is by itself an astonishing achievement, and more than sufficient to establish Wordsworth's greatness.

7. Principal Themes

Nature

As has often been observed, although the popular conception of Wordsworth is as the foremost of our 'nature poets' the poems themselves contain very little natural description. The reader who comes to Wordsworth's poetry expecting to find detailed pictorial representations of the landscape of the Lake District will be disappointed. In seeking to explain this apparent contradiction we should remember Wordsworth's own assertion that it is the 'Mind of Man' which is 'My haunt, and the main region of my song' (Preface to 'The Excursion', l. 40).

Wordsworth is interested not in the natural world but in the relationship between the natural world and the human consciousness. His poetry therefore offers us a detailed account of the complex interaction between man and nature – of the influences, insights, emotions and sensations which arise from this interaction – rather than a precise observation of natural phenomena. When a natural object is depicted it is usually apparent to us that the main focus of interest is the response of a human being (almost always Wordsworth himself) to that object. Indeed one of the most consistent concepts in Wordsworth is the idea that man and nature are inseparable; man exists not outside the natural world but as an active participant in it, so that 'nature' to Wordsworth means something that includes both inanimate and human nature – each is a part of the same whole. The moments of vision that are the source of some of Wordsworth's best poetry occur when he has a heightened sense of this unity. At such moments he responds not to the forms, shapes and colours of natural objects but to an inner force which permeates the natural world and which is felt within himself also.

Wordsworth was very interested in the *growth* of his relationship with nature – the ways in which it influenced him at different points in his life and the ways in which his awareness of it changed. One means of gaining a fuller sense of what nature meant to Wordsworth, and of the role that it played in his poetry, is to attempt to trace this growth, concentrating in our search upon the verse itself. Such an analysis might usefully begin with one of the central passages of 'Tintern Abbey'. After describing the scenery of the Wye valley and the influence that this has had upon him (a part of the poem to which we shall return) the mature poet reaches back into the past and recollects his younger self:

> when like a roe
> I bounded o'er the mountains, by the sides
> Of the deep rivers, and the lonely streams,
> Wherever nature led: more like a man
> Flying from something that he dreads than one
> Who sought the thing he loved. For nature then
> (The coarser pleasures of my boyish days,
> And their glad animal movements all gone by)
> To me was all in all, – I cannot paint
> What then I was. The sounding cataract
> Haunted me like a passion: the tall rock,
> The mountain, and the deep and gloomy wood,
> Their colours and their forms, were then to me
> An appetite; a feeling and a love,
> That had no need of a remoter charm,
> By thought supplied, nor any interest
> Unborrowed from the eye.

ll. 67–83

Here Wordsworth distinguishes between two phases in his developing relationship with nature. The first phase (chronologically) is referred to only parenthetically: '(The coarser pleasures of my boyish days,/ And their glad animal movements all gone by)'. Wordsworth's childhood experience of nature is of course evoked in much more detail elsewhere (particularly in the first two books of 'The Prelude'), but these two lines manage to suggest some of its most important characteristics. It was an experience in which satisfaction and enjoyment were derived from physical activity, and in which there was no conscious awareness of the natural world. 'Coarse' clearly suggests that the experience was, in some respects at least, inferior to what was to come later, while 'animal' similarly implies that a more refined, more fully human experience lay ahead. Most of the passage, however, concerns Wordsworth's youth. During this period his response to nature continued to be characterized by physical exuberance, but there was now an added *emotional* intensity. The sense of rapturous excitement is vividly conveyed, but in such a way as to suggest again that significant elements were missing from the experience. Thus while the assertion that nature 'To me was all in all' effectively evokes the strength of the young Wordsworth's passion for

99

natural objects, the very totality of this absorption is at the same time disturbing; it appears to exclude love of humanity and implies an ignorance of that invisible force, present within both human beings and nature, which was of such importance to the older Wordsworth. That he had only a limited perception of nature at this stage in his development is made more explicit later in the passage. He responded with his senses to the sounds, 'colours' and 'forms' of landscape, but the experience did not engage the intellect.

The poem continues to chart Wordsworth's developing attitude to nature, returning us to the present:

> That time is past,
> And all its aching joys are now no more,
> And all its dizzy raptures. Not for this
> Faint I, nor mourn nor murmur; other gifts
> Have followed; for such loss, I would believe,
> Abundant recompense. For I have learned
> To look on nature, not as in the hour
> Of thoughtless youth; but hearing often-times
> The still, sad music of humanity,
> Nor harsh nor grating, though of ample power
> To chasten and subdue. And I have felt
> A presence that disturbs me with the joy
> Of elevated thoughts; a sense sublime
> Of something far more deeply interfused,
> Whose dwelling is the light of setting suns,
> And the round ocean and the living air,
> And the blue sky, and in the mind of man:
> A motion and a spirit, that impels
> All thinking things, all objects of all thought,
> And rolls through all things.

ll. 83–102

In attempting to define the characteristics of this adult response to the natural world we might begin by noting that it incorporates human as well as inanimate nature. 'The still, sad music of humanity' clearly suggests a new sensitivity to human suffering. 'Music' also suggests something else, and in doing so anticipates the experience that is described in the concluding lines of the passage. It suggests *harmony*, and it is Wordsworth's ability to sense the interconnectedness of 'all things' – humanity, nature, 'All thinking things' and 'all objects of all thought' – that gives him the deepest satisfaction. He is able to penetrate beyond the external 'colours' and 'forms' of nature to the reality which is *in* nature, and in himself. The unity which Wordsworth senses is not inert but a vital, living force: 'A motion and a spirit' that 'impels' and 'rolls'. This profound awareness of the natural world's inner reality contrasts with the earlier enthusiastic enjoyment of the immediate pleasures of nature. The adult experience is more reflective, and while the growth of the intellect has brought its own kind of satisfaction this is revealingly described as a 'remoter charm' (l. 81). The development of the poet's relationship has thus involved a mixture of gain and loss; there is an element of regret in the recognition that the 'aching joys' and 'dizzy raptures' of youth are 'no more', and this is underlined by the effort of will evident in Wordsworth's assertion that he '*would* believe' that he has since found 'abundant recompense' for this loss.

Although 'Tintern Abbey' helps to clarify certain broad developments in Wordsworth's experience of nature, other poems, particularly 'The Prelude', make it equally clear that we should think of Wordsworth's changing perception of nature not in terms of rigidly separate stages but rather as a process of continuous growth, in which the accumulated feelings of the past always contribute to the experience of the present. Thus the beginnings of the adult Wordsworth's awareness of the essential unity of the universe can be found in formative childhood experiences, when this unity was revealed to him though not consciously understood. Although the poem 'There was a boy' is in the third person the experience it describes is clearly relevant here (the boy is in fact Wordsworth himself in an early manuscript, and in the Preface to *Poems in Two Volumes* he explains that in writing the poem he was 'guided by one of my own primary consciousnesses'). Excited by his ability to make owls respond to his mimic hootings, the boy revels in the 'concourse wild/ Of jocund din!' Occasionally, however, the boy's efforts would fail and there would be 'a pause/ Of silence such as baffled his best skill'. During such moments the boy would sometimes be surprised by a quieter, altogether more profound experience:

> *Then, sometimes, in that silence, while he hung*
> *Listening, a gentle shock of mild surprise*
> *Has carried far into his heart the voice*
> *Of mountain-torrents; or the visible scene*
> *Would enter unawares into his mind*
> *With all its solemn imagery, its rocks,*
> *Its woods, and that uncertain heaven received*
> *Into the bosom of the steady lake.*

ll. 18 25

The boy has a fleeting, intuitive sense of the vital forces of the natural world, forces which penetrate to the very centre of his being.

The skating episode in Book I of 'The Prelude' (ll. 452–89) describes a similar kind of experience. Here we see Wordsworth engaged in exhilarating physical activity (recalling the reference in 'Tintern Abbey' to the 'glad animal movements' of his boyhood):

> *I wheel'd about*
> *Proud and exulting, like an untired horse*
> *That cares not for his home.*

> ll. 458–60

As they sped along it seemed to the skaters that the surrounding cliffs moved with them. It was when Wordsworth suddenly 'Stopped short' that another moment of unexpected revelation occurred:

> *yet still the solitary Cliffs*
> *Wheeled by me – even as if the earth had roll'd*
> *With visible motion her diurnal round . . .*

> ll. 484–6

The human consciousness is captured here in active relationship with its natural surroundings. The apparent movement of the cliffs is a result of the boy's own movement; it is something created by his senses. But in another respect of course the motion of the cliffs is not an optical illusion at all; the earth is constantly revolving, and it is as if the boy can actually see this. As in 'There was a boy', he seems briefly to experience direct contact with an inner life force. Again the moment of vision is characterized by tranquillity:

> *Behind me did they stretch in solemn train*
> *Feebler and feebler, and I stood and watch'd*
> *Till all was tranquil as a dreamless sleep.*

> ll. 487–9

Although some of the most memorable passages in 'The Prelude' describe those occasions when Wordsworth experienced a sense of joyous communion with the natural world, in other episodes we see nature evoking a very different response – that of fear. This tension in Wordsworth's relationship with nature is significant, and is perhaps touched upon in the lines from 'Tintern Abbey' quoted earlier, when he recalled that as a youth he raced across the landscape

> *more like a man*
> *Flying from something that he dreads, than one*
> *Who sought the thing he loved.*

> ll. 70–72

Of his childhood years, Wordsworth says in 'The Prelude' that he was 'Foster'd alike by beauty and by fear' (Book I, l. 306). Relevant episodes here are those of the stolen boat (Book I, ll. 372–427), the theft of the trapped bird (Book I, ll. 309–32) and the raven's nest (Book I, ll. 333–50). On these occasions Wordsworth seems to have felt not so much harmony with the natural world as a disturbing sense of the *otherness* of nature (one critic, David Perkins, speaks of 'a suffering, almost panicky fear that man is doomed to isolation from the healthful influences of his natural surroundings'):

> *oh, at that time,*
> *While on the perilous ridge I hung alone,*
> *With what strange utterance did the loud dry wind*
> *Blow through my ears! the sky seem'd not a sky*
> *Of earth, and with what motion mov'd the clouds!*

> Book I, ll. 346–50

But fear could be a beneficent influence (as 'Foster'd' in the earlier quotation suggests), bringing its own kind of illumination. In the above passage the boy, although not yet capable of comprehending the significance of the experience, is beginning to realize that nature contains vital forces of which he had previously been unaware.

The notion of nature as educator extends to the moral sphere also. Again one of the clearest statements of Wordsworth's attitude is to be found in 'Tintern Abbey', where nature is identified as

> *The anchor of my purest thoughts, the nurse,*
> *The guide, the guardian of my heart, and soul*
> *Of all my moral being.*

> ll. 109–11

Earlier in the poem Wordsworth says that he has owed to the scenery of the Wye valley

> *feelings too*
> *Of unremembered pleasure: such, perhaps,*
> *As have no slight or trivial influence*

> *On that best portion of a good man's life,*
> *His little, nameless, unremembered, acts*
> *Of kindness and of love.*

ll. 30–35

Responding to the harmonious and 'beauteous forms' of nature can lead, as we have seen, to an awareness of the ultimate unity of all living things, and this in turn encourages sympathy and benevolence towards one's fellow human beings. Indeed, in 'The Excursion' Wordsworth uses the character of the Wanderer to argue that communion with the natural world *inevitably* has such an outcome:

> *For, the Man –*
> *Who, in this spirit, communes with the Forms*
> *Of nature, who with understanding heart*
> *Both knows and loves such objects as excite*
> *No morbid passions, no disquietude,*
> *No vengeance, and no hatred – needs must feel*
> *The joy of that pure principle of love*
> *So deeply, that, unsatisfied with aught*
> *Less pure and exquisite, he cannot choose*
> *But seek for objects of a kindred love*
> *In fellow-natures and a kindred joy.*
> *Accordingly he by degrees perceives*
> *His feelings of aversion softened down;*
> *A holy tenderness pervade his frame.*

Book IV, ll. 1207–20

Wordsworth's experience of nature can thus be seen as an evolving relationship which, by the time of 'Tintern Abbey' has reached a point where the poet is alive to the 'still, sad music of humanity' but alive also to the existence of a larger reality. The mature perception of the natural world has grown out of all that has preceded it. The childhood moments of vision (the implications of which are understood in recollection) have clearly been of crucial significance, but the 'aching joys' and 'dizzy raptures' of youth have played an important part also. In this latter period Wordsworth revelled in the sensory pleasures of nature, and was particularly captivated by its visual beauty ('the eye was master of the heart' – 'The Prelude', Book XI, l. 172). With time came a deeper understanding, but this understanding was arrived at only through the working of memory and intellect upon the sensory experiences of the past. Wordsworth's first visit to the Wye valley was during this phase of 'thoughtless' visual enjoyment, but he recognizes that it is partly to later reflection upon the sights he then observed that he owes those moments of supreme perception when he is able to 'see into the life of things' (ll. 35–49).

Earlier in the poem Wordsworth acknowledges yet another debt to his memories of the Wye valley:

> *These beauteous forms,*
> *Through a long absence, have not been to me*
> *As is a landscape to a blind man's eye:*
> *But oft, in lonely rooms, and 'mid the din*
> *Of towns and cities, I have owed to them,*
> *In hours of weariness, sensations sweet,*
> *Felt in the blood, and felt along the heart,*
> *And passing even into my purer mind,*
> *With tranquil restoration.*

ll. 22–30

We see here an additional element in Wordsworth's intimate involvement with the natural world. When he is faced by anxiety and depression nature offers him solace and is a source of regeneration. Confirmation of Wordsworth's belief in the consoling power of nature is provided by the solitaries. Characters such as the leech-gatherer, the Wanderer and the Old Cumberland Beggar live in such proximity to nature that they frequently seem to be extensions of the inanimate world (the leech-gatherer in 'Resolution and Independence', for example, is compared to a 'huge stone', a 'sea-beast' and a 'cloud'), and from this proximity they derive a strength and a stability that Wordsworth sometimes lacks. The solitaries have an awareness (not always conscious) of natural permanence which enables them to withstand individual human suffering; they can be said to represent an equipoise which Wordsworth strove towards but which, as the poems indicate, he had difficulty achieving.

This struggle is illustrated with particular vividness in 'Margaret, or The Ruined Cottage' (a poem later incorporated into Book I of 'The Excursion'). Significantly, the episode begins with the narrator not in harmony with his natural surroundings but discomforted by them. He toils with 'languid steps' across the 'slippery turf', trying vainly to disperse a group of insects gathered round his head (ll. 21–5). In contrast, the Wanderer when he is discovered resting peacefully upon a bench seems to merge effortlessly with the natural world:

105

> *Supine the Wanderer lay,*
> *His eyes as if in drowsiness half shut,*
> *The shadows of the breezy elms above*
> *Dappling his face.*

ll. 438–41

As the Wanderer tells the story of the former inhabitants of the ruined cottage (a pitiful tale of poverty, desertion and bereavement), the poet is deeply distressed. The Wanderer, however, though he has also been moved by Margaret's suffering, shows at the end of his story that he is able to overcome his sorrow at Margaret's individual fate because he is aware of a greater, transcendent reality, and of the essential continuity of life. To the Wanderer the cottage's overgrown garden is not a depressing symbol of decay but reassuring proof of the endlessly regenerative processes of nature:

> *I well remember that those very plumes,*
> *Those weeds, and the high spear-grass on that wall,*
> *By mist and silent rain-drops silvered o'er,*
> *As once I passed, into my heart conveyed*
> *So still an image of tranquillity,*
> *So calm and still, and looked so beautiful*
> *Amid the uneasy thoughts which filled my mind,*
> *That what we feel of sorrow and despair*
> *From ruin and from change, and all the grief*
> *That passing shows of Being leave behind,*
> *Appeared an idle dream.*

ll. 942–52

He finds comfort in the thought that Margaret is now part of this natural permanence: 'She sleeps in the calm earth, and peace is here' (l. 941).

A similar consolation is found in the Lucy poems. In 'A slumber did my spirit seal' the poet's grief at the girl's death is offset by the knowledge that she is now at one with the eternal forces of nature:

> *Rolled round in earth's diurnal course*
> *With rocks, and stones, and trees.*

ll. 7–8

And in 'Three years she grew' the girl is absorbed into nature through death, and shares

> *the silence and the calm*
> *Of mute insensate things.*

ll. 17–18

'Tintern Abbey', written in 1798, offers a broadly positive view of the poet's development, but in the Immortality Ode, begun in 1802 and finished in 1804, there is a more pessimistic account of human growth. The visionary power Wordsworth celebrated in the former poem was beginning to desert him, and there is now a sense of exclusion from the unity of the natural world. As has been seen, Wordsworth believed that the child's sense of oneness with nature had a directness and an immediacy unattainable in adult life. The Immortality Ode looks back to this childhood experience with a feeling of acute loss and emphasizes not the benefits of maturity but the way in which the intuitive knowledge of ultimate harmony is steadily eroded as we grow older. The poet still recognizes the outer beauty of the natural world but, cut off now from nature's inner life (an inner life to which in 'Tintern Abbey' the adult Wordsworth still had access), 'there hath past away a glory from the earth' (l. 18). In the concluding stanzas there is a determined effort to find 'Strength in what remains behind'; the insights of childhood are never wholly lost to us but retain some kind of existence in the memory. The heart of the poem, however, remains the earlier sense of extreme desolation, and we might feel that this desolation ominously foreshadows the decline in Wordsworth's creative powers; alienation from the vital forces of nature meant separation from the source of his imaginative life.

Imagination

The poets, critics and thinkers of the eighteenth century saw the imagination as an essentially passive faculty. Their beliefs were heavily influenced by the theories of the philosopher John Locke (1632–1704). He argued in 'An Essay Concerning Human Understanding' that the mind is in its original state blank (resembling 'white paper void of all characters') and then receives sense-impressions from outside: 'the objects of our senses ... obtrude their particular ideas upon our minds whether we will or no'. The imagination enables us to recall such sense-impressions and thus to reproduce objects in the mind when the objects themselves are absent. Thomas Hobbes defined imagination as 'nothing but *decaying*

107

sense', and declared that 'imagination and memory are but one thing, which for divers considerations has divers names'. The imagination was also thought capable of combining sense-perceptions in unusual ways so as to form objects that have no existence in reality. The chimera, an imaginary monster with a lion's head, a goat's body and a serpent's tail, is an illustration of this process. The mind's creativity did not therefore extend beyond the *rearrangement* of already existing elements of reality.

The Romantics, including Wordsworth, attributed much greater powers to the imagination and saw it as truly creative. Wordsworth recognized that our perception of the world partly comprises the passive registering of sense-impressions:

> *The eye – it cannot choose but see;*
> *We cannot bid the ear be still;*
> *Our bodies feel, where'er they be,*
> *Against or with our will.*

'Expostulation and Reply'

Our minds should not however be dominated by our senses. In 'The Prelude' Wordsworth recalls a period in his life when his perception of things was excessively dependent upon the faculty of sight:

> *The state to which I now allude was one*
> *In which the eye was master of the heart,*
> *When that which is in every stage of life*
> *The most despotic of our senses gain'd*
> *Such strength in me as often held my mind*
> *In absolute dominion.*

Book XI, ll. 171–6

Of more profound significance are those experiences in which the mind is pre-eminent:

> *those passages of life in which*
> *We have had deepest feeling that the mind*
> *Is lord and master, and that outward sense*
> *Is but the obedient servant of her will.*

Book XI, ll. 270–73

The mind has the capacity not merely to receive impressions of sight, sound, smell and so on but to interact with external objects so that our total perception of them is made up of what our faculties 'half create,/ And what perceive' ('Tintern Abbey'). This creative interchange with the external world begins in our earliest years; in 'The Prelude' Wordsworth describes the 'infant Babe' as

> *creator and receiver both,*
> *Working but in alliance with the works*
> *Which it beholds.*

Book II, ll. 273–5

According to Wordsworth, this imaginative power is 'the first/ Poetic spirit of our human life'. In most people it is 'abated or suppress'd' by the staleness and repetition of daily living, but in poets it is retained and developed. In 'The Prelude' he shows how during childhood his consciousness of the 'plastic power' that he possessed grew, as did his awareness of what it could achieve:

> *An auxiliar light*
> *Came from my mind which on the setting sun*
> *Bestow'd new splendour.*

Book II, ll. 387–9

The imagination is thus capable of acting upon external reality and creating thereby a different kind of reality.

In the Preface to the 1815 edition of his poems, Wordsworth explained that for him the word 'imagination' 'has no reference to images that are merely a faithful copy, existing in the mind, of absent external objects; but it is a word of higher import, denoting operations of the mind upon those objects'. It is through the operation of the poetic imagination upon it that the external world is invested with energy and life. Coleridge went so far as to assert that imagination 'is essentially vital, even as all objects (as objects) are essentially fixed and dead'. He also explained (in *Biographia Literaria*) Wordsworth's attempt to bring this dead world to life:

to give the charm of novelty to things of every day, and to excite a feeling analogous to the supernatural, by awakening the mind's attention from the lethargy of custom and directing it to the loveliness and the wonders of the world before us; an inexhaustible treasure, but for which, in consequence of the film of familiarity and selfish solicitude, we have eyes yet see not, ears that hear not, and hearts that neither feel nor understand.

For Wordsworth, the imagination is also the faculty that enables us to penetrate beyond the surface of the material world, to 'see into the life of things'. It is through the exercise of the imagination that we perceive the invisible connections of the universe and so become aware of its ultimate unity. This inner harmony is revealed to us through the medium of

109

nature, and before we reach the stage of greatest perception we respond to the external forms of nature with our senses. But if we progress from this to a genuine insight into the hidden reality of the natural world we reach a state which transcends the sensory and in which the operation of the senses is therefore suspended:

> *the light of sense*
> *Goes out in flashes that have shewn to us*
> *The invisible world . . .*

'The Prelude', Book VI, ll. 534–6

> *we are laid asleep*
> *In body, and become a living soul:*
> *While with an eye made quiet by the power*
> *Of harmony, and the deep power of joy,*
> *We see into the life of things.*

'Tintern Abbey'

A detailed account of the working of the imagination is given in the famous description of the ascent of Snowdon in Book XIII of 'The Prelude' (ll. 1–116). In this passage the climbing of a mountain parallels the ascent of the mind to a new peak of imaginative vision. Wordsworth and his friend Robert Jones went on a walking tour of North Wales in 1791, a year after their tour of France and Switzerland. Accompanied by a guide, they set out one night to watch the sun rise from the top of Snowdon. Initially, they travel through fog and mist and are absorbed in their own thoughts, their solitary musings disturbed only by the barking of their guide's dog when he discovers a hedgehog (ll. 1–35). Suddenly Wordsworth, who is ahead of the others, emerges from the clouds to discover the moon shining brightly overhead, illuminating a sea of mist below him (ll. 36–65). On this occasion, in place of the metaphorical gleams and flashes that are used elsewhere in Wordsworth's poetry to signify moments of revelation, there is a literal flash of light:

> *For instantly a Light upon the turf*
> *Fell like a flash: I look'd about, and lo!*
> *The moon stood naked in the Heavens . . .*

The moon dominates the mist beneath it, and the mist in turn prevails over the distant sea, which seemed 'To dwindle, and give up its majesty,/ Usurp'd upon as far as sight could reach'. From a gap in the clouds, a 'blue chasm', there could be heard 'the roar of waters, torrents, streams/ Innumerable'.

Later contemplation of the scene invests it with an emblematic significance (ll. 66–116). The scene resembles a human mind at the very height of its power; it is 'The perfect image of a mighty Mind,/ Of one that feeds upon infinity'. In exercising the imagination the mind draws on its own inner strength, on a mysterious 'underpresence' which is comparable to the 'dark deep thoroughfare' which was glimpsed in the midst of the clouds around Snowdon. Nature has further mirrored the working of the imagination by giving a demonstration of 'That domination which she oftentimes/ Exerts upon the outward face of things'. Nature is capable of influencing a scene in such a way as to make

> *one object so impress itself*
> *Upon all others, and pervade them so*
> *That even the grossest minds must see and hear*
> *And cannot chuse but feel.*

In this instance the view from Snowdon was dominated and transfigured by the moon, which created a scene of breathtaking grandeur. This power in nature is a 'genuine Counterpart' of the imagination, of 'the glorious faculty/ Which higher minds bear with them as their own'. The imagination has a similar capacity to impose order and unity upon the external world ('They from their native selves can send abroad/ Like transformations'). At the same time, when order and unity already exist they are immediately recognized by those in whom the imagination is highly developed ('whene'er it is/ Created for them, catch it by an instinct'). Such minds – by implication they belong to poets – can through the exercise of their imaginative power 'build up greatest things/ From least suggestions'. They are stimulated by sensory impressions but not 'enthralled' by them; rather, they see into the hidden life of things and 'hold communion with the invisible world'. Those with such minds, equipped as they are with a knowledge of ultimate harmony, are able to make sound 'moral judgements' and are the fortunate possessors of 'the highest bliss/ That can be known'.

8. Style

Wordsworth's poetry, when he is at his best, is inevitable, as inevitable as Nature herself. It might seem that Nature not only gave him the matter for his poem, but wrote his poem for him. He has no style.

Matthew Arnold's observation catches the essence of Wordsworth's poetic technique. The most striking characteristic of his style is that it is, on the face of it, peculiarly style-less. The lack of obvious literary artifice in Wordsworth's work, and his own emphasis on the importance of using language that is 'really spoken by men', should not however lead us to assume an absence of poetic craftsmanship. Dorothy's accounts of her brother's working methods, and his continual revision of his poetry, demonstrate that the simplicity and clarity we associate with Wordsworth were not achieved without deliberate and painstaking effort. It is Wordsworth's very ability so to conceal his technique that his language appears natural and unforced that makes his poetry art of the highest order.

A more detailed definition of Wordsworth's style might begin by noting those characteristics which it does *not* possess. In the Preface to the *Lyrical Ballads* (discussed in more detail in the next chapter) Wordsworth attacked the use of language that was unnecessarily elaborate and decorative. Such conventionally 'poetic' language was common in eighteenth-century verse, and he admitted that his refusal to employ diction of this kind had 'necessarily cut me off from a large portion of phrases and figures of speech which from father to son have long been regarded as the common inheritance of Poets'. Also absent from Wordsworth's verse is the kind of complex imagery associated most commonly with Shakespeare but found in many other poets also (the metaphysical poets of the seventeenth century, for example, and Keats and Hopkins in the nineteenth). He made use of metaphor and simile but his figurative language never has the dense suggestiveness of these other poets. Finally, he generally refrains from detailed pictorial descriptions of the natural world, again in contrast to Keats and also to many eighteenth-century poets. His preoccupation was with the fundamental workings of nature, and he found these most powerfully exhibited in the grandeur of mountains, seas and stars rather than in the finer particularities of landscape. Moreover, we almost never feel that

Wordsworth's intention is merely to hold up a mirror to nature; his poetry seeks to convey the impact (emotional and spiritual rather than sensory) that a natural scene has upon a human observer.

What Wordsworth's style aims at is absolute lucidity of expression. He uses language not to embroider experience but to record it; his language is selected with a view to reproducing particular experiences as faithfully as possible. His best poetry has a quality of simple but wonderfully vivid directness and clarity. Arnold, in the essay from which the opening quotation was taken, selected the following line from 'Michael' as an example of his 'true and most characteristic form of expression': 'And never lifted up a single stone.' Michael's emptiness and despair, reflected in his failure to complete the sheep-fold which symbolized the hope he had entrusted in his son, are made all the more moving by the bare simplicity with which they are described.

Another example of the effectiveness of Wordsworth's simple diction is this passage from 'Tintern Abbey':

> a sense sublime
> *Of something far more deeply interfused,*
> *Whose dwelling is the light of setting suns,*
> *And the round ocean and the living air,*
> *And the blue sky and in the mind of man:*
> *A motion and a spirit that impels*
> *All thinking things, all objects of all thought,*
> *And rolls through all things.*

Taken out of context, most of the key words here are unremarkable; by linking them with other words, however, their meaning and suggestiveness are enormously enhanced. Describing the ocean as 'round', for example, suggests that the life force that Wordsworth is attempting to define is of global dimensions. Similarly, the unusual use of 'living' to describe the air implies that this same life force can be felt all around us. Even more commonplace are the words 'all' and 'and', but by repeating these words Wordsworth suggests how apparently disparate elements of the world share an all-pervasive inner life.

In the following lines from 'There was a boy' the single word 'far' carries a similar power:

> *Then sometimes, in that silence, while he hung*
> *Listening, a gentle shock of mild surprise*
> *Has carried far into his heart the voice*
> *Of mountain-torrents . . .*

The word contributes much to our sense of the boy's profound communion with nature. Thomas de Quincey's admiration for this passage was such that he commented, 'The expression "far", by which space and its infinities are attributed to the human heart, and its capacities of re-echoing the sublimities of nature, has always struck me as with a flash of sublime revelation.'

Wordsworth's use of metaphor is marked by a similar avoidance of the obscure and the abstruse. Whereas with the metaphysical poets we find that, in Samuel Johnson's words, 'The most heterogeneous ideas are yoked by violence together' (John Donne, for example, wrote a poem in which a pair of lovers are compared to a set of compasses), Wordsworth's imagery has an opposite tendency; it does not seek to startle us but to match like with like. In view of his belief in the harmony of man and nature it is not surprising that most of his images are drawn from the natural world, thereby emphasizing the connections that exist between men and natural objects: the comparison of the leech-gatherer in 'Resolution and Independence' with a 'huge stone' and then with a 'sea-beast', for example, or the 'mild creative breeze' felt by the poet at the beginning of 'The Prelude', an inner breeze that is explicitly described as 'corresponding' to an outer one.

Wordsworth's deliberately unsophisticated style has had its critics. It has been argued with some justification that in certain of the *Lyrical Ballads* ('The Thorn', for example) the attempt to emulate ordinary speech results in language which too often lapses into banality. These occasional failures were perhaps an inevitable by-product of Wordsworth's attempt to circumvent the artificiality of much eighteenth-century poetry and bring language closer to ordinary human experience. His ultimate aim, however, was not simply to reproduce the language of casual conversation but, by using 'a *selection* of language really used by men', to give the illusion of everyday speech while retaining the profundity of ideas and intensity of feeling we expect of the finest poetry. Before it appears on the page, therefore, the language of his poems has been subjected to careful thought, selection and organization. Similarly, although he declares in the Preface that 'poetry is the spontaneous overflow of powerful feelings', he then adds, 'it takes its origin from emotion recollected in tranquillity'. During this process of tranquil recollection a subtle and refined poetic sensibility is brought to bear upon the original experience.

Wordsworth's theory of language did not, in practice, inhibit his vocabulary, and he did not balk at using complex words when necessary, as in the memorable description of ice-skating in 'The Prelude':

> *yet still the solitary cliffs*
> *Wheeled by me – as if the earth had rolled*
> *With visible motion her diurnal round!*

The word 'diurnal' has a weight and impressiveness that is perfectly suited to the evocation of a natural process that is awesome and mysterious (the word is used to similar effect in 'A slumber did my spirit seal'). He is also not afraid to admit that some experiences defy verbal definition. In the 'spots of time' passage in 'The Prelude' he recalls a formative childhood experience and admits

> *I should need*
> *Colours and words that are unknown to man*
> *To paint the visionary dreariness . . .*

Often the difficulty is one not only of communication but also of comprehension; on such occasions Wordsworth's language acknowledges his uncertainty as to the precise nature of what he has experienced. In the bird-nesting episode in 'The Prelude' the wind blew through the boy's ears 'With what strange utterance'; in the passage from 'Tintern Abbey' quoted earlier Wordsworth describes 'a sense sublime/ Of *something* far more deeply interfused'; in the Immortality Ode a tree and a field 'speak of something that is gone'.

Such honesty demonstrates Wordsworth's artistic integrity, an integrity that is one of the most consistent features of his poetry. The directness and simplicity of his style are to be valued because they reflect the openness of his nature. His poems speak to us from the heart. He is, in his own words, 'a man speaking to men', with impressive sincerity and candour.

9. The Poet as Critic

The central texts for a study of Wordsworth's critical opinions are the 1798 Advertisement to *Lyrical Ballads*, the Preface that accompanied the second edition in 1800, and the revised version of this Preface that appeared in 1802. In these writings Wordsworth sought to explain (and defend against criticism) his own poetic practice, which is why his critical views are of such interest to the reader of his poetry. The thoughts of the critic give us a valuable insight into the methods, intentions and preoccupations of the poet.

According to the 1800 Preface, the aim of the poems in *Lyrical Ballads* was to trace 'the primary laws of our nature'. In the 1802 version, Wordsworth further argues that the object of poetry is 'truth, not individual and local, but general and operative'. The belief that all human beings are fundamentally alike, and that poetry should concern itself with the general and permanent truths of human nature, is frequently asserted in eighteenth-century literary criticism (Samuel Johnson, for example, maintained that 'Nothing can please many, and please long, but just representations of general nature'). For Wordsworth, the essential elements of the human character are best exemplified by those who lead a simple rural existence, people whose natures have not been distorted by the artificialities of city life. The subject-matter of the *Lyrical Ballads* therefore comprises 'incidents and situations from common life':

Low and rustic life was generally chosen because in that situation the essential passions of the heart find a better soil in which they can attain their maturity, are less under restraint, and speak a plainer and more emphatic language; because in that situation our elementary feelings exist in a state of greater simplicity and consequently may be more accurately contemplated and more forcibly communicated.

Wordsworth's views on the language that poets should use are a natural consequence of this interest in simple country life. The elaborate diction of many eighteenth-century poets is to be condemned because it is so unlike the language of ordinary human experience. Its artificiality prevents a convincing representation of general human truths, of the 'primary laws of our nature'. Instead, the language of ordinary speech is to be favoured because it is the language 'really used by men'. In particular, the language of rustic life is to be admired for its lack of adornment and because a rural environment encourages the development of a language that expresses the permanent truths of our nature:

The language too of these men is adopted (purified indeed from what appear to be its real defects, from all lasting and rational causes of dislike or disgust) because such men hourly communicate with the best objects from which the best part of language is originally derived; and because, from their rank in society and the sameness and narrow circle of their intercourse, being less under the action of social vanity they convey their feelings and notions in simple and unelaborated expressions. Accordingly such a language arising out of repeated experience and regular feelings is a more permanent and a far more philosophical language than that which is frequently substituted for it by Poets.

In practice, while simplicity of language is certainly one of the hallmarks of Wordsworth's style, he did not seek to reproduce in his poems the colloquial diction used by rustics. Wordsworth is not a folk or dialect poet. The 1802 Preface gives a clearer indication of his poetic technique when it refers to 'a selection of the language really spoken by men', a selection which will 'entirely separate the composition from the vulgarity and meanness of ordinary life'. Wordsworth's language draws upon that of everyday speech, but it is free of regional variations and while it may appear to have the naturalness of ordinary conversation it is the product of careful creative effort.

In the Preface, Wordsworth develops his belief in using the language of ordinary people by arguing that the language of poetry should not differ from that of prose. The poet should avoid language which is specifically poetic; he should not employ a diction 'peculiar to him as an individual Poet or belonging simply to Poets in general'. Wordsworth realizes that he is inviting the question, 'Why, professing these opinions, have I written in verse?' and this leads to a discussion of the advantages of metre, which is seen as the only distinguishing feature between poetry and prose. He begins with a general assertion that metre invests writing with an additional 'charm', but then gives a more complex account of the purposes that metre serves:

The end of Poetry is to produce excitement in coexistence with an overbalance of pleasure. Now, by the supposition, excitement is an unusual and irregular state of the mind; ideas and feelings do not in that state succeed each other in accustomed order. But if the words by which this excitement is produced are in themselves powerful, or the images and feelings have an undue proportion of pain connected with them, there is some danger that the excitement may be carried beyond its proper bounds. Now the co-presence of something regular, something to which the mind has been accustomed when in an unexcited or a less excited state, cannot but have great efficacy in tempering and restraining the passion by an intertexture of ordinary feeling.

117

The regularity of metre restrains and controls the excitement of passion, enabling us to endure what might otherwise be unendurable. With any art form it is important that we should be at a certain distance from the emotions represented. Metre further helps to create this distance by making us more conscious of the distinction between art and reality; metre has a tendency 'to divest language in a certain degree of reality, and thus to throw a sort of half consciousness of unsubstantial existence over the whole composition'. Wordsworth illustrates his point by arguing that the most moving passages in Samuel Richardson's novel *Clarissa* cause us to feel real distress, while 'Shakespeare's writings, in the most pathetic scenes, never act upon us as pathetic beyond the bounds of pleasure' – something which is to a large degree a result of 'small, but continual and regular impulses of pleasurable surprise from the metrical arrangement'. At the same time, although metre tempers passion it also plays a part in arousing it, and if a poet has failed by other means to achieve the intended emotional response 'metre will greatly contribute to impart passion to the words'.

In the 1802 Preface, Wordsworth also addresses himself to the question, 'What is a Poet?' Just as he rejected the use by poets of a specialized language that set them apart from others, so in answering this question he stresses the poet's role as a representative of common humanity; he is 'a man speaking to men'. He is different from other people, however, in that he lives life more intensely; the potentialities of the human character are more fully developed in him. The poet is a man

endued with more lively sensibility, more enthusiasm and tenderness, who has a greater knowledge of human nature, and a more comprehensive soul, than are supposed to be common among mankind; a man pleased with his own passions and volitions, and who rejoices more than other men in the spirit of life that is in him.

He also of course has superior powers of expression, but Wordsworth emphasizes that in all these respects the poet does not differ 'in kind from other men, but only in degree'.

Although the poet should concern himself with the general truths of human nature, Wordsworth accepts that his poems will often be rooted in personal experience. Indeed, his famous definition of poetry as 'the spontaneous overflow of powerful feelings' suggests a belief in the value of self-expression that is characteristically Romantic. This does not however conflict with the poet's essential purpose, because his 'passions and thoughts and feelings are the general passions and thoughts and feelings of men'. Wordsworth gives in the Prefaces a detailed and illuminating description of the process by which these experiences are turned into poetry. When he refers to poetry as a 'spontaneous overflow' of feeling he does not mean that it should be an uncontrolled outpouring of emotion. A period of disciplined contemplation is essential to the creation of the best poetry:

Poems to which any value can be attached, were never produced on any variety of subjects but by a man who being possessed of more than usual organic sensibility had also thought long and deeply. For our continued influxes of feeling are modified and directed by our thoughts . . .

The creative process is, initially at least, a meditative one; it usually begins with the recollection of a past emotional experience:

Poetry . . . takes its origin from emotion recollected in tranquillity: the emotion is contemplated till by a species of reaction the tranquillity gradually disappears, and an emotion, similar to that which was before the subject of contemplation, is gradually produced, and does itself actually exist in the mind. In this mood successful composition generally begins, and in a mood similar to this it is carried on.

Poetic activity thus involves the exercise of the imagination as well as of the memory. The poet must recreate the experience to the point where he seems almost to be reliving it. The original and recollected emotions are however 'similar' rather than wholly identical. This is because the original feeling has now been 'modified' by thought. This interaction of thought and feeling is a continuous process that begins as soon as the original experience has occurred. As time passes the significance of the experience is assessed and it is related to other experiences the poet has had. When he attempts to recollect it in order to write a poem – and this may be years later – the process of selection, modification and evaluation continues. Eventually thought and emotion combine to produce the 'spontaneous overflow of powerful feelings' that characterizes the best poetry. The word 'spontaneous' here suggests that while a creative state of mind is partly the result of conscious and disciplined endeavour it is not entirely achieved by an effort of will. The unconscious – the part of the mind that 'The Prelude' calls an 'underpresence' – also has an essential contribution to make.

Wordsworth's theory of poetic composition cannot be said to hold true for all poetry, but it greatly enhances our understanding of his own work. The best of his poems – works such as 'Tintern Abbey', 'Resolution and Independence' and 'The Prelude' – are distinguished by a unique blend of emotional intensity and intellectual profundity. They are a triumphant vindication of the belief that poetry originates from 'emotion recollected in tranquillity'.

Bibliography

Editions

The Poetical Works of William Wordsworth (5 volumes), edited by Ernest de Selincourt and Helen Darbishire (Clarendon Press, 1959)

William Wordsworth: The Poems (2 volumes), edited by John O. Hayden (Penguin, 1977)

The Prelude (1805), edited by Ernest de Selincourt and Stephen Gill (Oxford University Press, 1970)

The Prelude: A Parallel Text (1805 and 1850), edited by J. C. Maxwell (Penguin, 1979)

The Prelude, 1799, 1805, 1850, edited by Jonathan Wordsworth, M. H. Abrams and Stephen Gill (W. W. Norton, 1979)

The Prose Works of William Wordsworth (3 volumes), edited by W. J. B. Owen and Jane Worthington Smyser (Clarendon Press, 1974)

Biography

MOORMAN, MARY *William Wordsworth: A Biography* (2 volumes) (Clarendon Press, 1957 and 1965)

Background reading

BUTLER, MARILYN *Romantics, Rebels and Reactionaries: English Literature and its Background, 1760–1830* (Oxford University Press, 1981)

FORD, BORIS (ed.) *From Blake to Byron: Pelican Guide to English Literature*, Volume 5 (Penguin, 1957)

HILL, JOHN SPENCER (ed.) *The Romantic Imagination: A Casebook* (Macmillan, 1977)

PRICKETT, STEPHEN (ed.) *The Context of English Literature: The Romantics* (Methuen, 1981)

WILLEY, BASIL *The Eighteenth-Century Background* (Chatto & Windus, 1940)

WORDSWORTH, DOROTHY *Journals of Dorothy Wordsworth* (2 volumes), edited by Ernest de Selincourt (Macmillan, 1941)

Critical studies

BATESON, F. W. *Wordsworth: A Re-interpretation* (Longman, 1954)

BEER, JOHN *Wordsworth and the Human Heart* (Macmillan, 1978)

121

Masterstudies: The Poetry of William Wordsworth

BEER, JOHN *Wordsworth in Time* (Faber, 1979)

FERRY, DAVID *The Limits of Mortality* (Wesleyan University Press, 1959)

HARTMANN, GEOFFREY H. *Wordsworth's Poetry 1784–1814* (Yale University Press, 1964)

HARVEY, W. J. and GRAVIL, RICHARD (eds.) *Wordsworth: 'The Prelude': A Casebook* (Macmillan, 1972)

HOUGH, GRAHAM *The Romantic Poets* (includes chapter on Wordsworth and Coleridge) (Hutchinson, 1953)

JONES, ALUN R. and TYDEMAN, WILLIAM (eds.) *Wordsworth: 'Lyrical Ballads': A Casebook* (Macmillan, 1972)

LEAVIS, F. R. *Revaluation* (includes essay on Wordsworth) (Chatto & Windus, 1936)

MCMASTER, GRAHAM (ed.) *William Wordsworth: A Critical Anthology* (Penguin, 1972)

PERKINS, DAVID *The Quest for Permanence: The Symbolism of Wordsworth, Shelley and Keats* (Harvard University Press, 1959)

PIRIE, DAVID *William Wordsworth: The Poetry of Grandeur and of Tenderness* (Methuen, 1982)

ROSSITER, A. P. *Angel with Horns* (includes lecture on 'Wordsworth and Shakespeare') (Longman, 1961)

SALVESEN, CHRISTOPHER *The Landscape of Memory: A Study of Wordsworth's Poetry* (Edward Arnold, 1965)

FOR THE BEST IN PAPERBACKS, LOOK FOR THE

PENGUIN BOOKS OF POETRY

American Verse
Ballads
British Poetry Since 1945
Caribbean Verse
A Choice of Comic and Curious Verse
Contemporary American Poetry
Contemporary British Poetry
Eighteenth-Century Verse
Elizabethan Verse
English Poetry 1918–60
English Romantic Verse
English Verse
First World War Poetry
Georgian Poetry
Irish Verse
Light Verse
London in Verse
Love Poetry
The Metaphysical Poets
Modern African Poetry
Modern Arab Poetry
New Poetry
Poems of Science
Poetry of the Thirties
Post-War Russian Poetry
Spanish Civil War Verse
Unrespectable Verse
Victorian Verse
Women Poets

FOR THE BEST IN PAPERBACKS, LOOK FOR THE

PENGUIN REFERENCE BOOKS

The Penguin English Dictionary

Over 1,000 pages long and with over 68,000 definitions, this cheap, compact and totally up-to-date book is ideal for today's needs. It includes many technical and colloquial terms, guides to pronunciation and common abbreviations.

The Penguin Reference Dictionary

The ideal comprehensive guide to written and spoken English the world over, with detailed etymologies and a wide selection of colloquial and idiomatic usage. There are over 100,000 entries and thousands of examples of how words are actually used – all clear, precise and up-to-date.

The Penguin English Thesaurus

This unique volume will increase anyone's command of the English language and build up your word power. Fully cross-referenced, it includes synonyms of every kind (formal or colloquial, idiomatic and figurative) for almost 900 headings. It is a must for writers and utterly fascinating for any English speaker.

The Penguin Dictionary of Quotations

A treasure-trove of over 12,000 new gems and old favourites, from Aesop and Matthew Arnold to Xenophon and Zola.

FOR THE BEST IN PAPERBACKS, LOOK FOR THE 🐧

PENGUIN REFERENCE BOOKS

The Penguin Guide to the Law

This acclaimed reference book is designed for everyday use, and forms the most comprehensive handbook ever published on the law as it affects the individual.

The Penguin Medical Encyclopedia

Covers the body and mind in sickness and in health, including drugs, surgery, history, institutions, medical vocabulary and many other aspects. 'Highly commendable' – *Journal of the Institute of Health Education*

The Penguin French Dictionary

This invaluable French-English, English-French dictionary includes both the literary and dated vocabulary needed by students, and the up-to-date slang and specialized vocabulary (scientific, legal, sporting, etc) needed in everyday life. As a passport to the French language, it is second to none.

A Dictionary of Literary Terms

Defines over 2,000 literary terms (including lesser known, foreign language and technical terms) explained with illustrations from literature past and present.

The Penguin Map of Europe

Covers all land eastwards to the Urals, southwards to North Africa and up to Syria, Iraq and Iran. Scale – 1:5,500,000, 4-colour artwork. Features main roads, railways, oil and gas pipelines, plus extra information including national flags, currencies and populations.

The Penguin Dictionary of Troublesome Words

A witty, straightforward guide to the pitfalls and hotly disputed issues in standard written English, illustrated with examples and including a glossary of grammatical terms and an appendix on punctuation.

FOR THE BEST IN PAPERBACKS, LOOK FOR THE

PENGUIN MASTERSTUDIES

This comprehensive list, designed to help advanced level and first-year undergraduate studies, includes:

SUBJECTS
Applied Mathematics
Biology
Drama: Text into Performance
Geography
Pure Mathematics

LITERATURE
Dr Faustus
Eugénie Grandet
The Great Gatsby
The Mill on the Floss
A Passage to India
Persuasion
Portrait of a Lady
Tender Is the Night
Vanity Fair
The Waste Land

CHAUCER
The Knight's Tale
The Miller's Tale
The Nun's Priest's Tale
The Pardoner's Tale
The Prologue to The Canterbury
   Tales
A Chaucer Handbook

SHAKESPEARE
Hamlet
King Lear
Measure for Measure
Othello
The Tempest
A Shakespeare Handbook

'Standing somewhere between the literal, word-by-word explication of more usual notes and the abstractions of an academic monograph, the Masterstudies series is an admirable introduction to mainstream literary criticism for A Level students, in particular for those contemplating reading English at university. More than that, it is also a model of what student notes can achieve' – *The Times Literary Supplement*

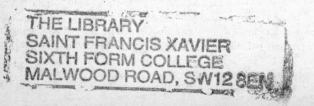